Winning TOEFL

Speaking Step 2

Wit&Wisdom

Wit&Wisdom is the professional language publishing company of the PAGODA Education Group.

Winning TOEFL Speaking Step 2

Published by Wit&Wisdom
Wit&Wisdom is the professional language publishing company of the
PAGODA Education Group.
19F, PAGODA Tower, 419, Gangnam-daero,
Seocho-gu, Seoul, 06614, Rep. of KOREA
www.pagodabook.com

First published 2009
Seventh impression 2021
Printed in the Republic of Korea

ISBN 978-89-6281-064-6 (13740)

Publisher ǀ Ru-Da Go
Writer   ǀ PAGODA Language Education Center

A defective book may be exchanged at the store where you purchased it.

Winning TOEFL iBT

Speaking Step 2

Introduction to iBT TOEFL

iBT TOEFL (internet-based TOEFL) is designed to measure how well non-native speakers of English read, listen, speak, and write in English. The test has four sections: reading, listening, speaking, and writing. Each section of the test is worth 30 points and the highest possible score on the iBT is 120 points (30 points x 4 sections). Most questions are worth 1 point each, but some of the questions in each section are worth more than 2 points.

 **→ For more information, visit the ETS website (www.ets.org).**

Speaking Section

In the speaking section, there are a total of 6 different types of tasks. Therefore, test takers will be asked to answer 6 tasks in 20 minutes. The first two tasks are independent tasks that involve only speaking. The other four tasks are integrated tasks, in which the test taker is required to answer the question based on only the listening passage or both the reading and listening passages.

		Process	Time
Independent Task	Task 1 (Opinion)	Speaking	Preparation time: 15 sec Response time: 45 sec
	Task 2 (Opinion)	Speaking	Preparation time: 15 sec Response time: 45 sec
Integrated Task	Task 3 (Campus situation topic)	Reading Listening Speaking	Reading time: 45 sec Preparation time: 30 sec Response time: 60 sec
	Task 4 (Academic course topic)	Reading Listening Speaking	Reading time: 45 sec Preparation time: 30 sec Response time: 60 sec
	Task 5 (Campus situation topic)	Listening Speaking	Preparation time: 20 sec Response time: 60 sec
	Task 6 (Academic course topic)	Listening Speaking	Preparation time: 20 sec Response time: 60 sec

It is also important to know the description of each task in order to understand the point.

Task Description

Task	Description
Task 1 (Personal Opinion)	Asked to answer personal opinion on, for example, favorites, persons, characteristics, etc
Task 2 (Preference, Agree/Disagree)	Asked to choose between two contrasting choices or to ask whether the test taker agrees or disagrees on the matter
Task 3 (Fit & Explain)	• **Reading:** Announcement or notice in regard to a campus situation • **Listening:** Two students' dialogue related to the reading passage • **Speaking:** To state one of the speaker's opinion within the context of the reading passage and the dialogue
Task 4 (General/Specific)	• **Reading:** Brief explanation on general terms • **Listening:** Academic lecture which deals with more specific explanation or examples of the term in the reading • **Speaking:** To explain what is meant by the term using both reading and listening passages
Task 5 (Problem Solving)	• **Listening:** Two students' dialogue related to a problem and two possible solutions that can happen in a campus situation • **Speaking:** To briefly mention the problem and solutions mentioned in their dialogue, and to choose one of the solutions that a test taker thinks is better
Task 6 (Summary)	• **Listening:** Academic lecture which deals with the explanation of the term or concept and gives examples to support the term • **Speaking:** To summarize the lecture and show a thorough understanding

Winning TOEFL Speaking series

This is the second speaking book in the *Winning TOEFL* series. It consists
of eight units and an actual test. Each unit is divided into two tasks:
an independent task and an integrated task. Each task in every unit is
classified in a different color. The independent task is in green and the
integrated task is in orange. Both tasks include one practice section and
one test section. This book is for beginner-level students, so it is slightly
easier than the original passages seen on the actual TOEFL.

**Each unit consists of two big tasks and each task consists of four big
sections individually. Each section has the following subsections:**

Independent Task	Integrated Task
Introduction Target iBT TOEFL Questions	**Introduction** Target iBT TOEFL Question
⬇	⬇
Key Expressions Key Expressions → Let's Pratice	**Key Expressions** Key Expressions → Let's Pratice
⬇	⬇
Practice Get Started → Get Ready → Speak Up	**Practice** Get Started → Get Ready → Speak Up
⬇	⬇
Test iBT TOEFL Question	**Test** iBT TOEFL Question

Each section has the following subsections:

Introduction

Target iBT TOEFL Question

This part introduces what types of question students will deal with in this unit. Each unit focuses on the following types of iBT TOEFL speaking questions:

		Types of Questions
Unit 1	Independent Task Integrated Task	Task 1 (Asking personal opinion on favorites) Task 5 (Campus-related problem solving)
Unit 2	Independent Task Integrated Task	Task 1 (Asking personal opinion on favorites) Task 5 (Campus-related problem solving)
Unit 3	Independent Task Integrated Task	Task 1 (Asking personal opinion on persons) Task 6 (Summary of academic lecture)
Unit 4	Independent Task Integrated Task	Task 1 (Asking personal opinion on characteristics) Task 6 (Summary of academic lecture)
Unit 5	Independent Task Integrated Task	Task 2 (Choosing between the two) Task 3 (Campus-related pros and cons)
Unit 6	Independent Task Integrated Task	Task 2 (Choosing between the two) Task 3 (Campus-related pros and cons)
Unit 7	Independent Task Integrated Task	Task 2 (Agreeing or disagreeing) Task 4 (Explanation of the term mentioned in the lecture from general to specific)
Unit 8	Independent Task Integrated Task	Task 2 (Agreeing or disagreeing) Task 4 (Explanation of the term mentioned in the lecture from general to specific)
Actual Test	Task 1~6	

Key Expressions

This is the first part of the task. Students are provided with some key expressions that should be learned in advanced to complete the task. With those key expressions in mind, students are asked to do **Let's Practice**. This can be done individually or with a partner depending on circumstances.

Practice

(1) Get Started

This part functions as a warming-up activity. This helps students to understand new words and expressions that will be used in order to do the next part. Students are asked to do most of the vocabulary activities and have some fun at the beginning.

(2) Get Ready

Independent Task

This part functions as a guiding activity that helps the student to answer the iBT TOEFL question. Students are required to ask and answer some light questions that are all related to the iBT TOEFL question. These questions and **Practice Speaking** boxes are to encourage students to closely follow the sample response.

Integrated Task

This part functions as a guiding activity that helps the student to answer the iBT TOEFL question. Students are required to perform a dictation, note-taking and some comprehension checking. These questions and **Practice Speaking** boxes are to encourage students to closely follow the sample response.

(3) Speak Up

Students are asked to combine all of the responses they have learned in **Practice Speaking** boxes. They should be able to reach the ideal response due to the guided processes they have gone through.

Check Your Response

A sample response has been recorded by native speakers. Students are asked to listen to this sample response and to take notes on this. This will help students with both their listening and note-taking skills.

Test

This is the last part of the task. Students are given an iBT TOEFL question and are asked to create their own response. Provided with some idea tips and key expressions, students are encouraged to make an outline and create their own response. They are asked to time how long it takes to answer the question.

Actual Test

Six tasks are provided as an actual test. The test questions contain longer reading and listening passages that are similar to the real iBT TOEFL questions, so that students will be able to have an overall view on the real iBT TOEFL questions.

Contents

Independent Task
Favorites I

•• Target iBT TOEFL Question

Independent Task

Speaking

What is your favorite sport or game?
Explain why this is your favorite. Include details and
examples to support your explanation.

Integrated Task
Problem Solving

•• Target iBT TOEFL Question

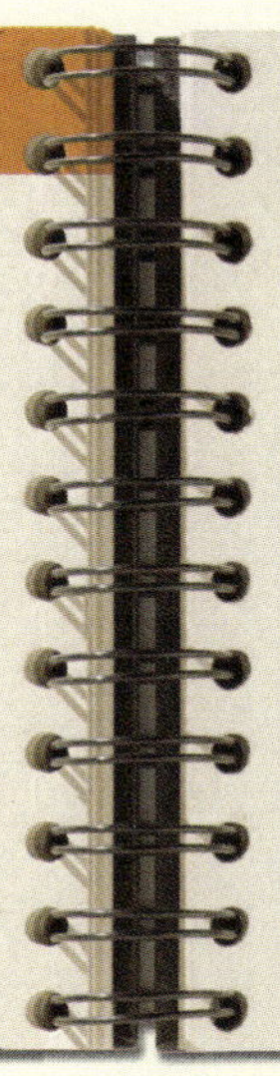

Integrated Task

Listening-Speaking

The students discuss two possible solutions to the man's problem. Describe the problem. Then state which of the two solutions you prefer and explain why.

Key Expressions

My favorite ... is ...

> **e.g.** My favorite music is R & B.

> **e.g.** My favorite book is *The Little Prince*.

I like / love to V ... = I like V-ing ...   (V = Verb)

> **e.g.** I like to learn about different cultures. = I like learning about different cultures.

> **e.g.** I love to play soccer with my friends. = I love playing soccer with my friends.

First, / Secondly,

> **e.g.** First, / Secondly, the music makes me relaxed.

That's why ...

> **e.g.** That's why my favorite music is hip-hop.

> **e.g.** That's why I like to read cartoons.

Let's Practice

1. Jazz is my favorite music.
   = ____________________________ is Jazz.

2. First of all, I like to hear the sound of the saxophone.
   = ____________ , I like ____________ .

3. Another reason is that I love listening to live music.
   = ____________ , I love to ____________ .

4. That's why my favorite music is Jazz.
   = ____________ I like to ____________ .

Get Started

Choose the word from the box that best completes the sentence.

- tournament
- patience
- competitive
- strategies
- endurance

1 Perfect team _____________ will help the team win the game.

2 My friends and I like to do some _____________ sports together.

3 The World Cup is the biggest soccer _____________ in the world.

4 I lost my _____________ when he yelled at me.

5 Swimming is one of the sports that helps build up _____________.

Get Ready

Ⓐ Answer the following question.

What is your favorite sport or game?

➡ My favorite sport / game is ⬚⬚⬚⬚⬚⬚ .

• soccer	• basketball	• baseball	• tag	• hide-and-seek
• hiking	• badminton	• inline skating	• board games	

Ⓑ Why do you like to play that sport or game? Check (✔) two reasons. You may add your own answer.

- ▢ It is fun and exciting.
- ▢ I like to play sports with lots of people.
- ▢ I am good at playing ⬚⬚⬚⬚⬚ .
- ▢ I like to watch the World Cup / the Olympics / tournaments.
- ▢ I like something competitive.
- ▢ It is good for my health.
- ▢ ⬚⬚⬚⬚⬚ .

Practice Speaking

My favorite sport / game is ⬚⬚⬚⬚⬚

There are two reasons why ⬚⬚⬚⬚⬚ is my favorite.

First, ⬚⬚⬚⬚⬚

Secondly, ⬚⬚⬚⬚⬚

C Write down the two reasons you have chosen in **B**. Then using the idea tip below as a guide, add specific details to support your two reasons. You may add your own experiences or examples to support your reasons.

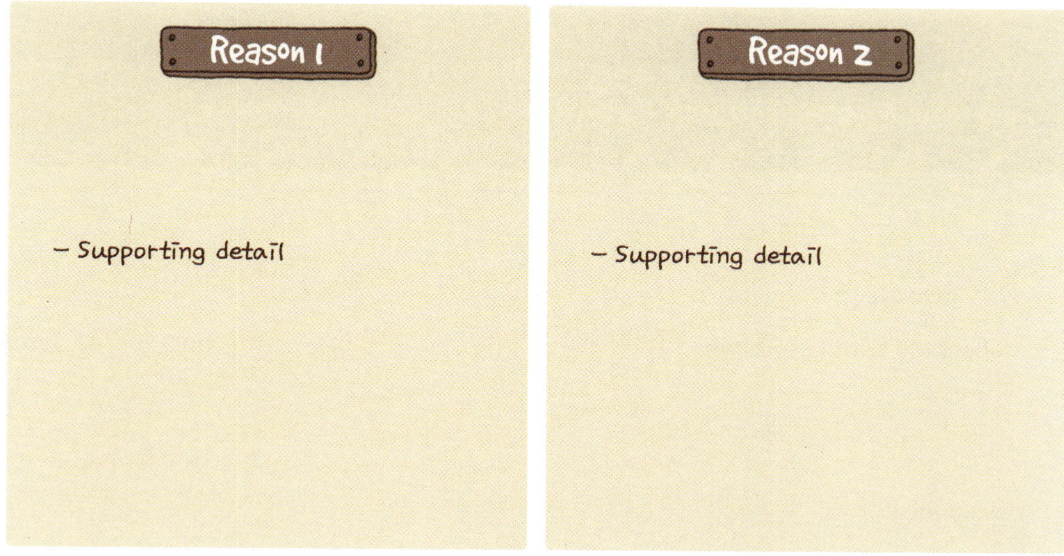

Idea Tip

- can build up endurance and patience
- can develop team strategies because it is a multi-player sport
- thrilled with excitement when I win the game
- like to watch the biggest tournament in the world
- people from all over the world cheer for their countries all summer
- helps me to relieve stress

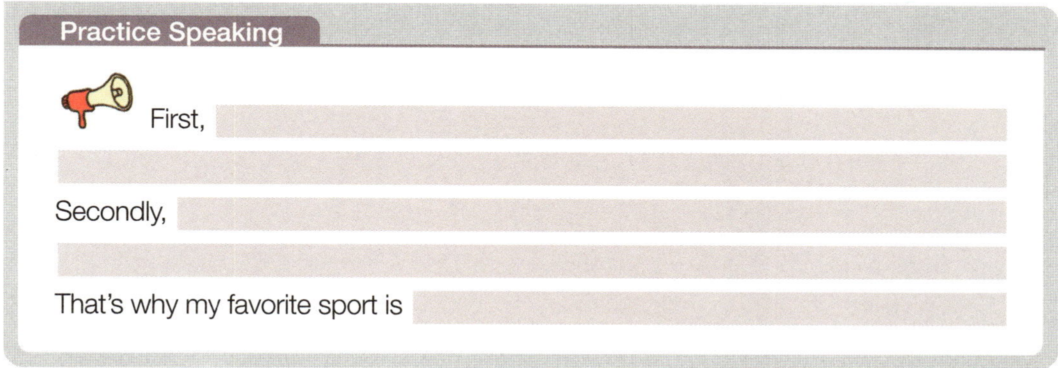

Practice Speaking

First,

Secondly,

That's why my favorite sport is

Speak Up 

Referring from Ⓐ to Ⓒ, make your response to the question below.

What is your favorite sport or game? Explain why this is your favorite. Include details and examples to support your explanation.

My favorite sport / game is ____________________

There are two reasons why ____________________ is my favorite. First,
____
____

Secondly, ____________________
____
____

That's why my favorite sport / game is ____________________

Check Your Response 

🔊 01_U1_1.mp3

Listen to the sample response and try to take some notes.

• Favorite sport or game:

Reason 1:

- Supporting detail:

Reason 2:

- Supporting detail:

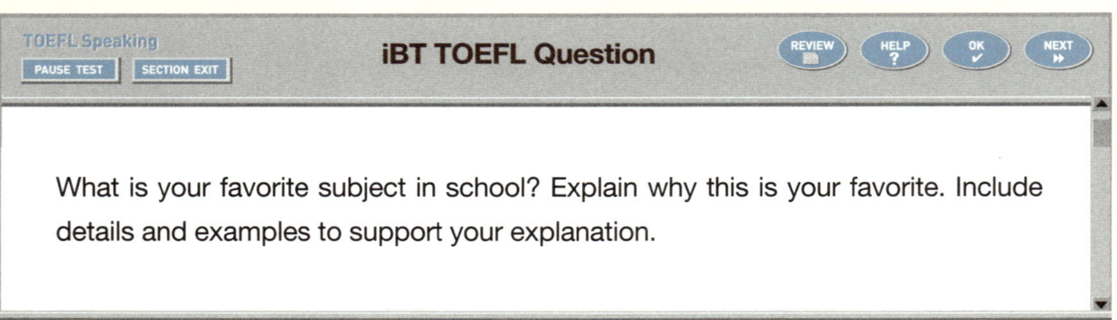

A Using the ideas below as a guide to find two major reasons, complete the outline for a response.

- [ ] I love to learn about the lives of our ancestors.
- [ ] It is important to know what has been done in the past.
- [ ] I am good at playing instrument / sport.
- [ ] It is the most exciting time in school.
- [ ] I love numbers.
- [ ] I love reading literatures.
- [ ] I like the teacher.
- [ ] I don't have to think hard.
- [ ] I like challenge.

Outline

- **Favorite Subject:**

  Reason 1:

  Reason 2:

  – Supporting detail:

  – Supporting detail:

B Referring to your outline, create your own response to the question using the key expressions below. Make sure you time while you speak.

- My favorite subject in school is ...
- There are two reasons why ...
- First, ...
- Secondly, ...
- That's why ...

How long did it take for you to answer the question?

Response time:

Key Expressions

- **The man/woman's problem is that ...**

  e.g. The man's problem is that he cannot attend the meeting.

  e.g. The woman's problem is that she finds the class very difficult.

- **One is that ... / The other is that ...**

  e.g. One / The other is that he could talk about the problem with his roommate.

- **I think the ... is better.**

  e.g. I think the second solution is better.

- **First of all, ... / Second of all, ...**

  e.g. First / Second of all, he can miss the morning class if he stays up late.

Let's Practice

Problem

The woman has a doctor's appointment on the day of her field trip.

Solutions

1. Tell her teacher that she can't go.
2. Ask her doctor to change the date.

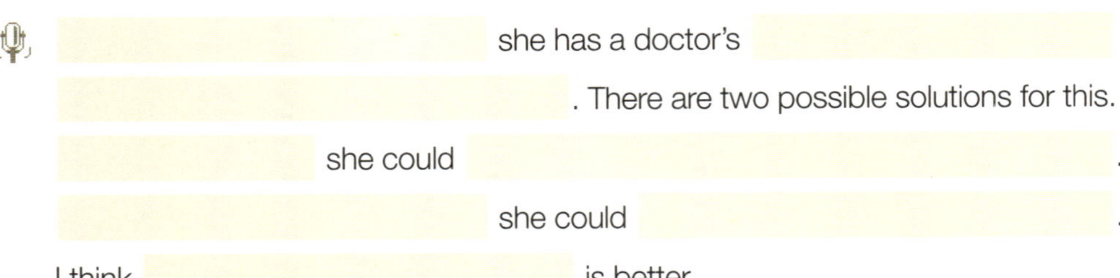

                   she has a doctor's   . There are two possible solutions for this.   she could   .   she could   . I think   is better.

Get Started

Choose the word from the box that best completes the sentence.

> • stressed out • difficult • fall behind
> • mistake • drop • harm

1 Today is the last day that I can ______ the Physics course.

2 If I feel that I ______ in physics class, I try hard to catch up.

3 I get so ______ when my roommate turns on loud music at night.

4 Forgetting to bring your textbook one time will do no ______ to your grade.

5 I think the violin is ______ to learn in the beginning.

6 It was my biggest ______ that I hadn't been to the dentist before.

A-1 Listen to two students talking about Chemistry class. Fill in the blanks to complete the dialogue.

)) 02_U1_2.mp3

W: Hey, you look really stressed out! What's going on?

M: Oh... It's this Chemistry class that ①____________ me out. It's too ②____________ for me. It's only the second week and I'm already ③____________ ④____________ .

W: Is it really that bad?

M: Yes! I have ⑤____________ idea what's going on. I think it was a ⑥____________ to take this course. What am I going to do?

W: Well, you could ⑦____________ the course. If you think of your ⑧____________ , it's better not to keep ⑨____________ it. You'll lose a bit of ⑩____________ , but it's better than getting a low grade. That will ⑪____________ your GPA.

M: Yeah. I've thought of that. The problem is that I'll end up losing about a ⑫____________ dollars. That's not a small amount of money.

W: Hmm... Then, how about this? Get some ⑬____________ from others. You could get extra help from the ⑭____________ , or join a ⑮____________ group. There are many ways of getting ⑯____________ help.

M: I thought about it, but I don't know many people, and the professor seems very ⑰____________ .

W: I'm sure your professor would be happy to answer your ⑱____________ .

A-2 **Answer the following questions.**

1 Why is the man so stressed out?

    Ⓐ because he finds it difficult to keep up in Chemistry class

    Ⓑ because he regrets causing trouble in Chemistry class

2 What **two** possible solutions does the woman suggest to the man?

    Ⓐ that he could get a private tutor

    Ⓑ that he could drop the course

    Ⓒ that he could get extra help from others

    Ⓓ that he could retake the course next semester

Practice Speaking

The man's problem is that

The woman suggests two possible solutions. One is that

The other is that

)) 03_U1_3.mp3

• Man's problem:

Solution 1:

Solution 2:

– Detail:

– Detail:

B-2 Answer the following questions.

1 Which solution do you think is better?

    □ **Solution 1** (go to number 2)   □ **Solution 2** (go to number 3)

2 Why do you think the first option is better? Choose **two** reasons why you think so.

    □ There's a limit on getting help from others.
    □ He will risk failing the course.
    □ Losing a hundred dollars is better than getting an F.

3 Why do you think the second option is better? Choose **two** reasons why you think so.

    □ It is a waste of money to drop the class.
    □ A study group can be very helpful and effective.
    □ It is good to challenge himself with something he finds difficult.

C Check (✔) which solution you think is better and write down the two reasons you have chosen in **B-2**. Then add specific details to support your two reasons.

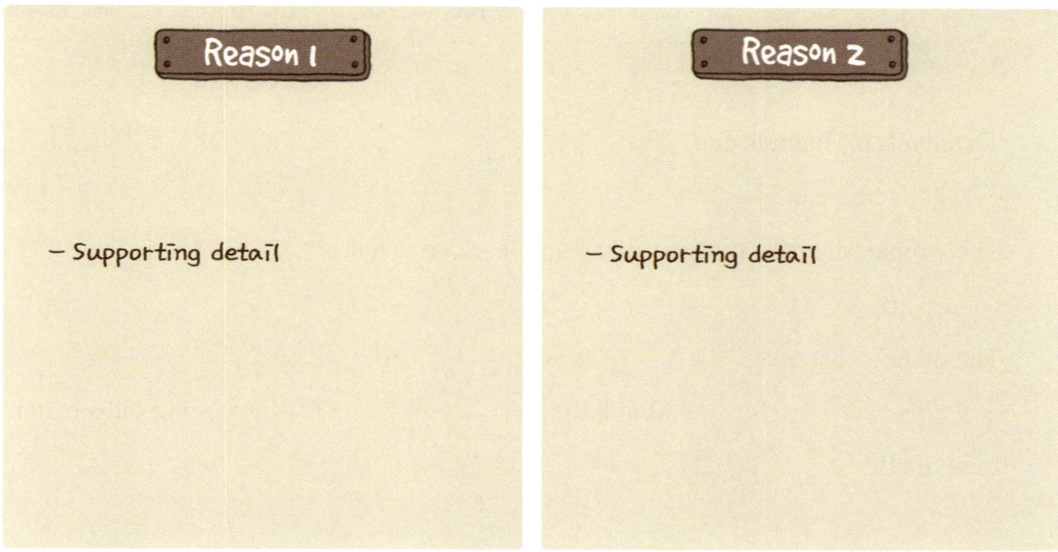

Practice Speaking

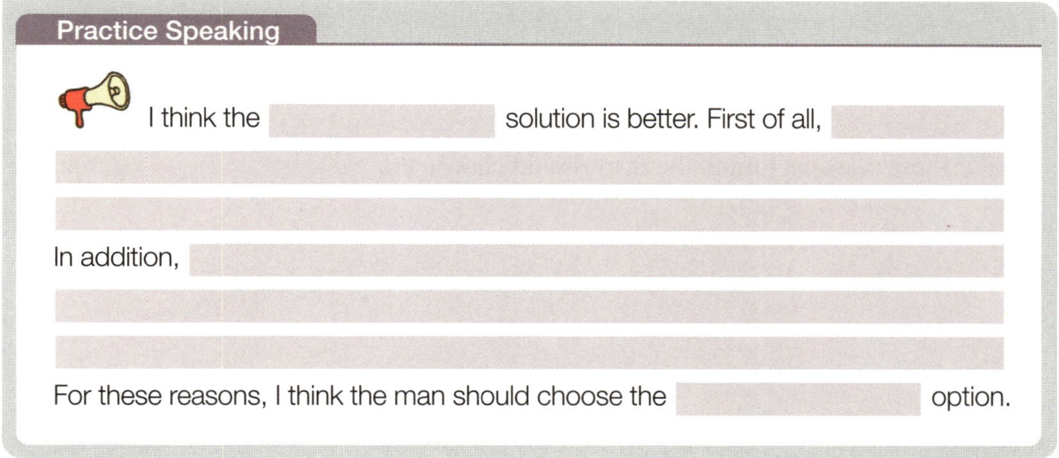

I think the ______ solution is better. First of all, ______

______

______

In addition, ______

______

______

For these reasons, I think the man should choose the ______ option.

UNIT 1

Speak Up

Referring from Ⓐ to Ⓒ, make your response to the question below.

> The students discuss two possible solutions to the man's problem. Describe the problem. Then state which of the two solutions you prefer and explain why.

The man's problem is that

The woman suggests two possible solutions. One is that

The other is that

I think the   solution is better.

First of all,

In addition,

For these reasons, I think the man should choose the   option.

  04_U1_4.mp3

Listen to the sample responses and complete the notes below.

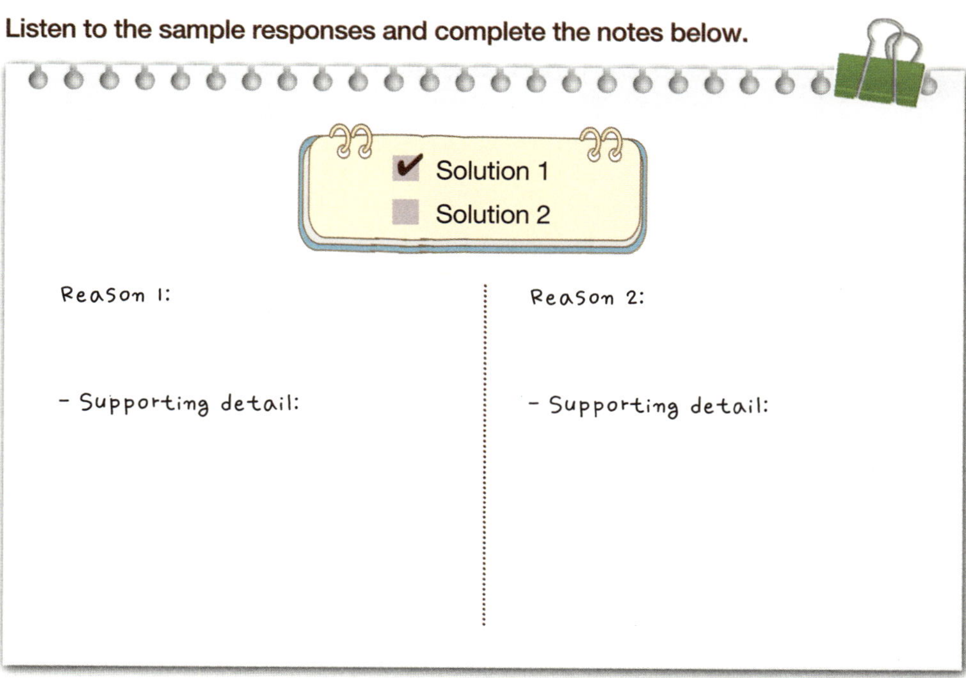

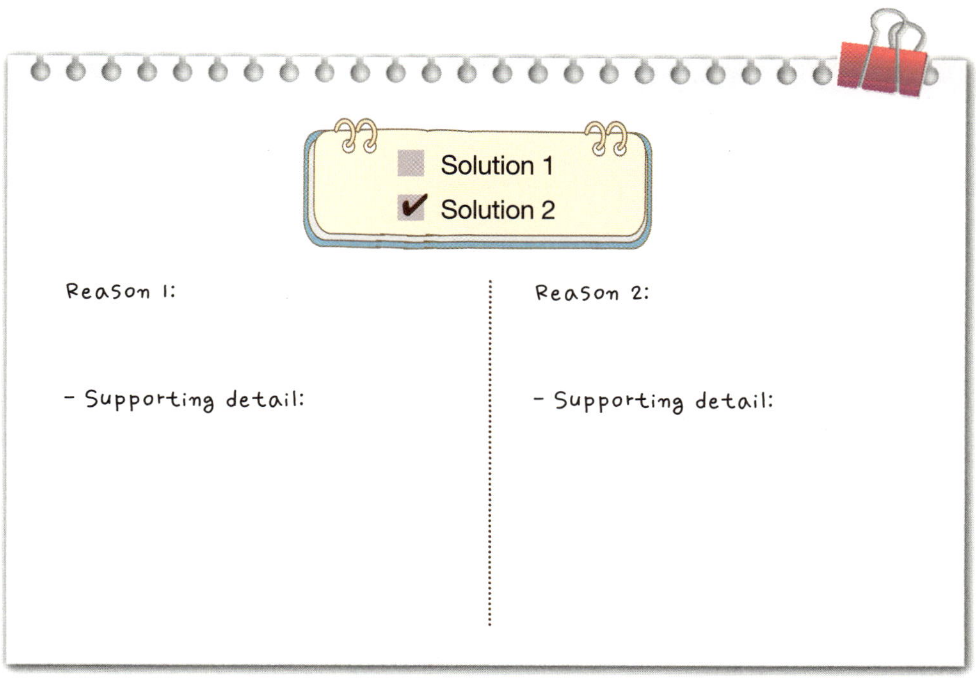

A

🔊 05_U1_5.mp3

Listen to two students talking about the woman's problem. Take notes while you are listening.

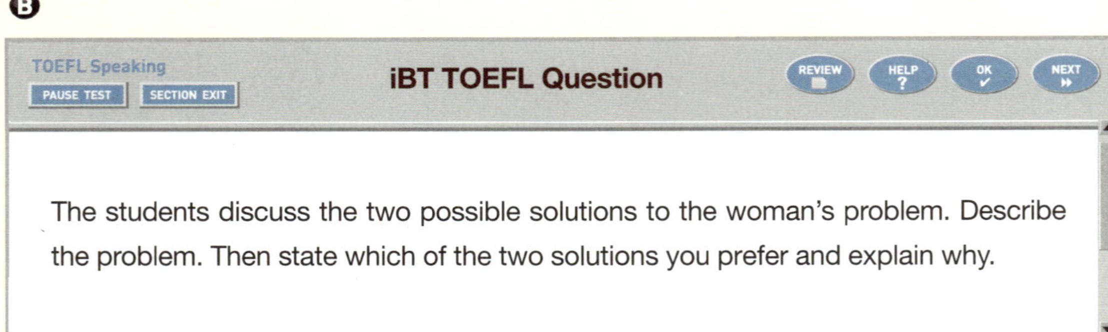

B

The students discuss the two possible solutions to the woman's problem. Describe the problem. Then state which of the two solutions you prefer and explain why.

Referring to the notes in **A**, complete the outline below for a clear response.

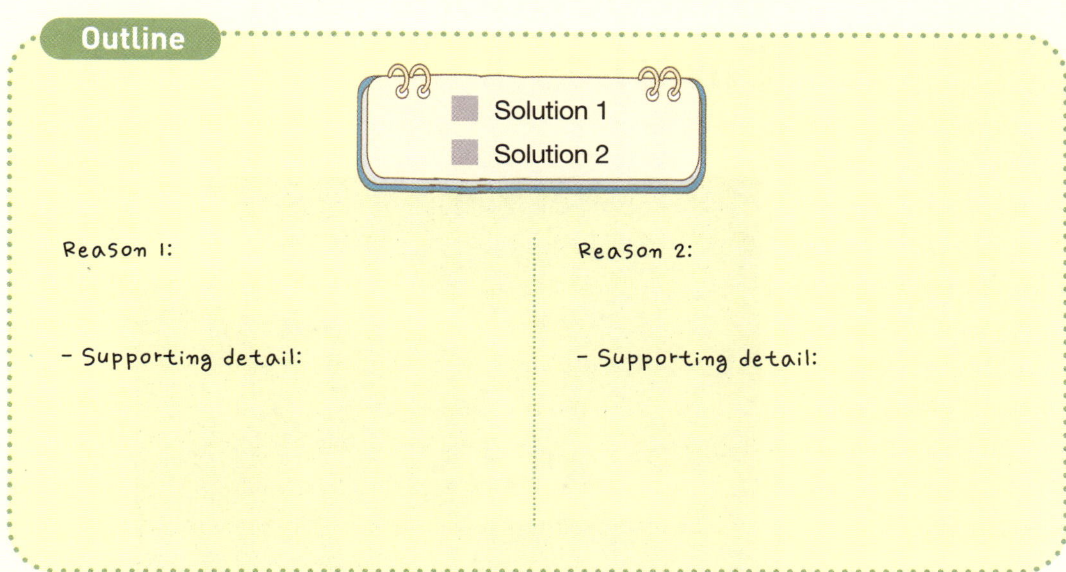

C Referring to your outline, create your own response to the question using the key expressions below. Make sure you time while you speak.

Key Expressions

- The woman's problem is that ...
- The man suggests two solutions. One is that ... The other is that ...
- I think ...
- First of all, ...
- Second of all, ...
- For these reasons, ...

How long did it take for you to answer the question?

Response time:

Independent Task
Favorites Ⅱ

•• Target iBT TOEFL Question

Independent Task

Speaking

What is your favorite movie genre?
Explain why you like this genre. Include details and
examples to support your explanation.

Integrated Task
Problem Solving

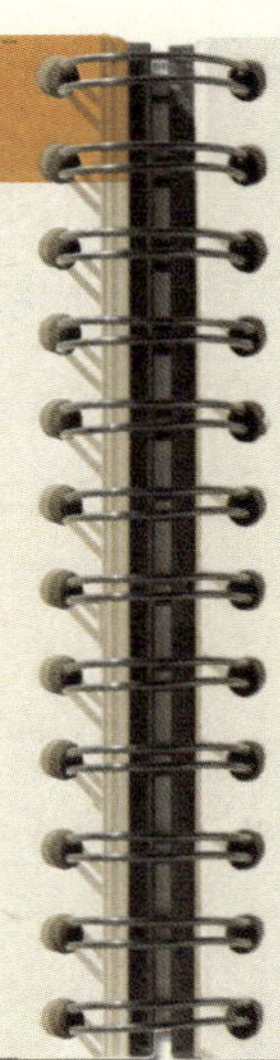

•• Target iBT TOEFL Question

Integrated Task

Listening-Speaking

The students discuss two possible solutions to the woman's problem. Describe the problem. Then state which of the two solutions you prefer and explain why.

Key Expressions

○ **I would have to say that my favorite ... is ...**

> **e.g.** I would have to say that my favorite kind of music is hip-hop.

> **e.g.** I would have to say that my favorite book is *Charlie and the Chocolate Factory*.

○ **S + V ... when S + V ...**   (S=Subject, V=Verb)

> **e.g.** I watch cartoons. → never get bored

> ⇒ I never **get** bored **when I watch** cartoons.

> **e.g.** I was 10. → learned piano

> ⇒ I **learned** piano **when I was** 10.

○ **The first / second reason is that ...**

> **e.g.** The first / second reason is that my teddy bear means a lot to me.

Let's Practice

1. I guess my favorite city is New York.

   = ________________________________.

2. I arrived. → nobody was there

   = ________________________________.

3. I watch movies at home. → fall asleep

   = ________________________________.

4. First, there are lots of museums and historical places to see.

   = The ________________________________

Get Started ••

Choose the word from the box that best completes the sentence. Change form where necessary.

- imaginary
- keep one on the edge of one's seat
- brave
- stunt
- sweat

1 Being a _______________ person involves high risk and danger.

2 I don't show fear in difficult situations because I am _______________.

3 After he ran 100 meters, his T-shirt was soaked with _______________.

4 When I'm bored, I often talk to my _______________ friend.

5 The action movie I watched yesterday _______________ throughout the entire movie.

Get Ready

Ⓐ Answer the following question.

What is your favorite movie genre?

⇒ I would have to say that my favorite movie genre is   .

• action	• comedy	• horror
• fantasy	• romance	• animation

Ⓑ Why do you like that movie genre? Check (✔) two reasons. You may add your own answer.

☐ I like funny / scary / imaginary storylines.

☐ Time flies when I watch   movies.

☐ It helps to relieve stress.

☐ I like to prove that I am brave enough to watch horror films.

☐ I like to put myself into the character's position.

☐ I like to watch actors or actresses perform stunts.

☐   .

Practice Speaking

📢 I would have to say that my favorite movie genre is

There are two reasons why   is my favorite genre.

The first reason is that

The second reason is that

C Write down the two reasons you have chosen in B. Then using the idea tip below as a guide, add specific details to support your two reasons. You may add your own experiences or examples to support your reasons.

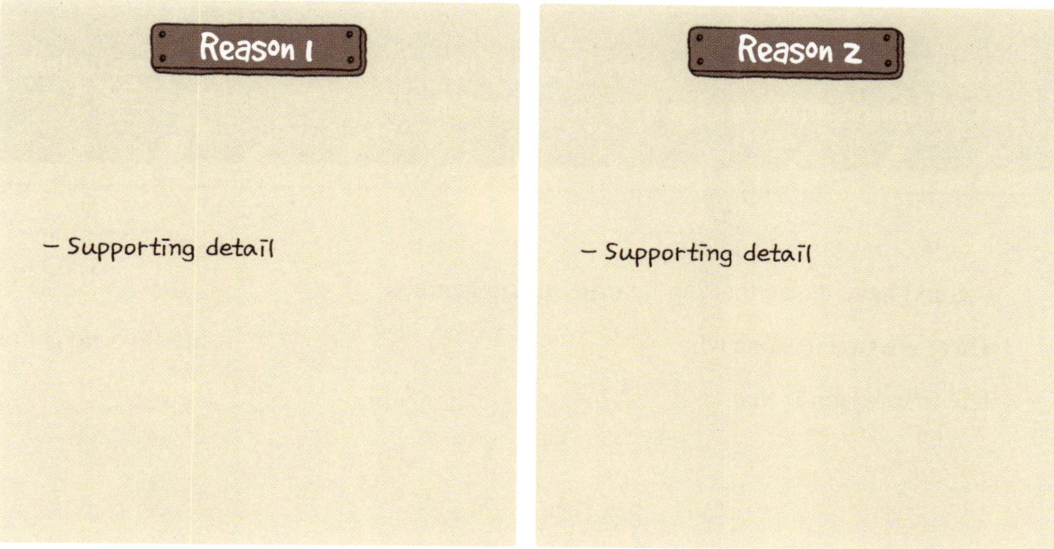

Idea Tip

- so exciting that they keep me on the edge of my seat
- so amazing
- can focus only on movies
- like to guess what happens next
- imagine what I would do if I were
- make me sweat with fear / emotion

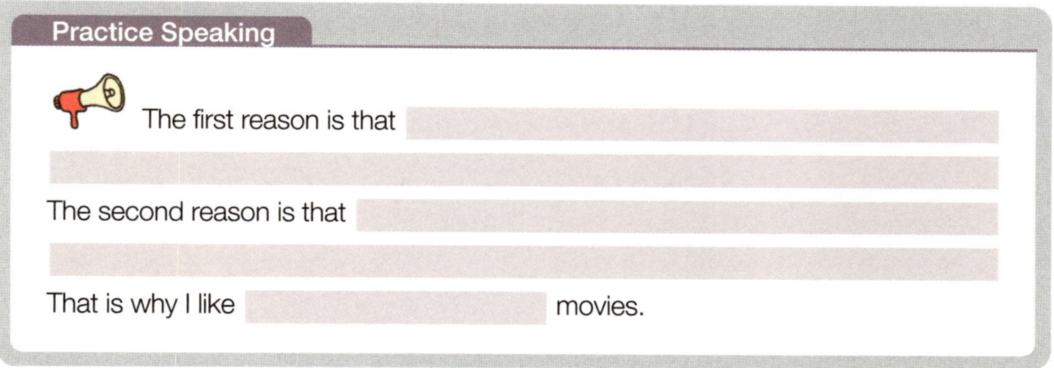

Speak Up

Referring from Ⓐ to Ⓒ, make your response to the question below.

What is your favorite movie genre? Explain why you like this movie genre. Include details and examples to support your explanation.

I would have to say that my favorite movie genre is

There are two reasons why   is my favorite genre.

The first reason is that

The second reason is that

That's why I like   movies.

Listen to the sample response and try to take some notes.

- Favorite movie genre:

  Reason 1:

  - Supporting detail:

  Reason 2:

  - Supporting detail:

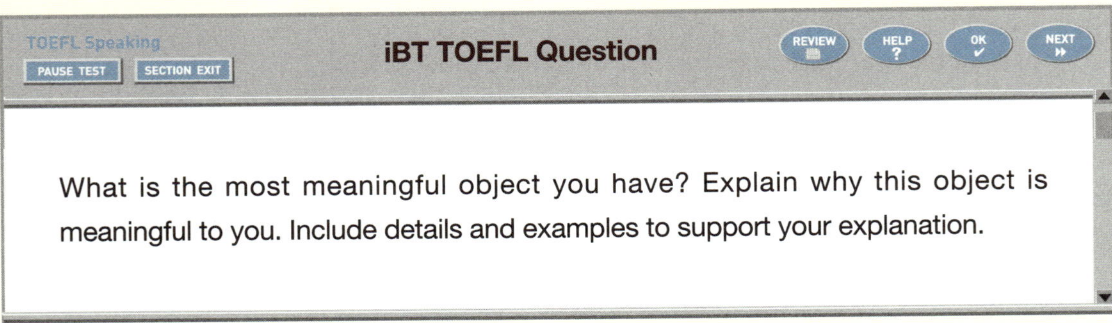

Ⓐ Using the ideas below as a guide to find two major reasons, complete the outline for a response.

☐ It has lots of memories.

☐ ________________________ gave it to me as a gift.
(name of someone)

☐ It reminds me of ________________.
(name of someone)

☐ It is the most expensive / oldest object I have.

☐ It is very rare and is worth a lot of money now.

☐ It is the first object I bought for myself.

☐ I carry it everywhere I go.

Outline

• The most meaningful object:

Reason 1:   Reason 2:

  – Supporting detail: – Supporting detail:

B Referring to your outline, create your own response to the question using the key expressions below. Make sure you time while you speak.

- I would have to say that the most meaningful object I have is ...
- There are two reasons why ...
- The first reason is that ...
- The second reason is that ...
- That is why ...

How long did it take for you to answer the question?

Response time:

Integrated Task - Problem Solving

o could either ... or ...

  e.g. He **could either** take the subway **or** ask his friends for a ride.

  e.g. She **could either** talk about the problem with her roommate **or** change rooms.

o If S + V ... , S will ...　　　　　　　　(S=Subject,　V=Verb)

  e.g. get up late tomorrow → be in trouble

    ⇨ **If** I **get up** late tomorrow, I **will** be in trouble.

o V -ing ... + V ... = To V ... + V ...　　　　　(V=Verb)

  e.g. **Exercising is** very important to stay healthy.

    = **To exercise is** very important to stay healthy.

  e.g. **Watching** the news **helps** children develop their knowledge.

    = **To watch** the news **helps** children develop their knowledge.

o These are the reasons that I think ...

  e.g. **These are the reasons that I think** the first option is better.

  e.g. **These are the reasons that I think** the man should choose the second option.

Let's Practice

1. One option is that she could go to bed early and wake up early.
   The other is that she could stay awake all night.

   = She could ________________________________

   ________________________________ .

2. go to bed late and get up late → definitely miss the morning class

   : If ________________________ , ________________________ .

3. To study English is not that easy.

   = ________________________ is ________________________ .

Get Started

Choose the word from the box that best completes the sentence.

- irresponsible
- rest
- give up
- important
- on time
- concentrate

1 Only two students followed the schedule and the ______ of the students stayed behind.

2 I finished my project right ______, so I didn't lose any marks.

3 The bad things about him are that he is disorganized and ______.

4 It is very ______ that students read many books.

5 People should never ______ before they really try their best.

6 It is hard to ______ on my studies when there's a construction going on.

Get Ready

A-1 Listen to two students talking about a study group assignment. Fill in the blanks to complete the dialogue.

)) 07_U2_2.mp3

M: Are you coming to the ① ________ tonight?

W: I really want to, but I'm not sure yet.

M: Why? What's wrong?

W: I'm in this study group, and there's a ② ________ ③ ________ that I have to do by ④ ________ . There's no way I can finish it all by tomorrow anyway. If I don't finish the reading, they're going to think I'm ⑤ ________ and ⑥ ________ .

M: I bet that if you just ⑦ ________ the party and really work hard, you might get it done ⑧ ________ time.

W: Hmm... But I don't think that's going to be ⑨ ________ . It's really too much.

M: I don't think your group members will think you are irresponsible if you try your ⑩ ________ . Why don't you do the ones that are most ⑪ ________ first? And then, if you have time, you can do the ⑫ ________ .

W: Yeah... I'm trying, but I'm not sure. Right now, all I can think about is the party.

M: Well... If you can't get it done either way, why don't you just ⑬ ________ yourself? ⑭ ________ the people in your study group and tell them that you won't be able to do it, and just come to the party! I don't think you'll be able to ⑮ ________ well anyways.

W: Yeah, but I don't think they'll be happy about it.

M: Of course they won't be too happy about it, but at least you can have fun and get a good night's sleep.

1 What is the woman so stressed about?

    Ⓐ She has to finish some reading for her study group by tomorrow, but she also wants to go to a party tonight.

    Ⓑ She does not want anybody to think of her as irresponsible and lazy.

2 Which **two** possible solutions does the man suggest to the woman?

    Ⓐ that she could just go to bed early

    Ⓑ that she could go to the party and pretend that she has done the reading assignment

    Ⓒ that she could stay home and stay up late to finish the reading

    Ⓓ that she could tell her study group members that she can't make it and just enjoy the party

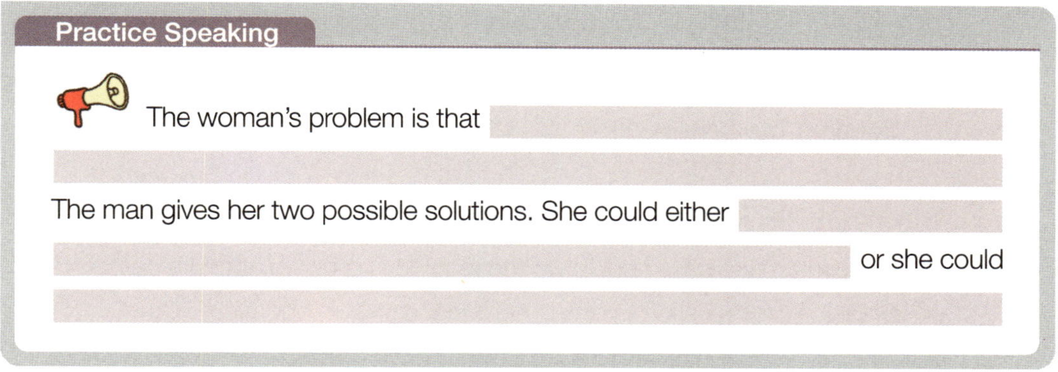

Practice Speaking

The woman's problem is that

The man gives her two possible solutions. She could either

or she could

🔊 08_U2_3.mp3

• Woman's problem:

Solution 1:

Solution 2:

– Detail:

– Detail:

B-2 Answer the following questions.

1 Which solution do you think is better?

☐ **Solution 1** (go to number 2)   ☐ **Solution 2** (go to number 3)

2 Why do you think the first option is better? Choose **two** reasons why you think so.

☐ It doesn't make sense not to do the reading in order to attend a party.

☐ Breaking promises for a party shows that she is irresponsible.

☐ There is a difference between not trying and not doing.

3 Why do you think the second option is better? Choose **two** reasons why you think so.

☐ It is impossible for her to finish the reading, so she should just have fun instead.

☐ She should do what she really likes.

☐ It will be a waste of time doing the reading.

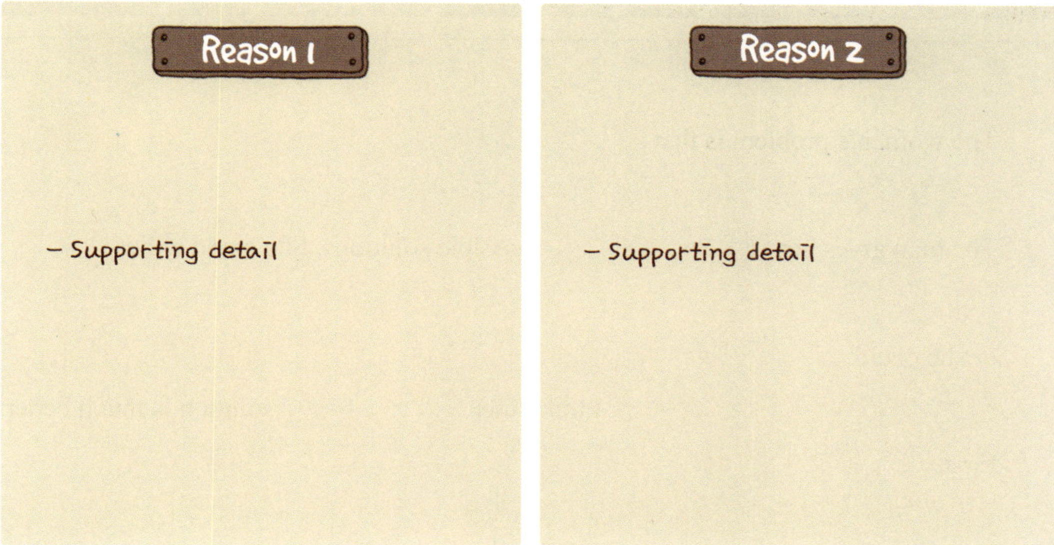

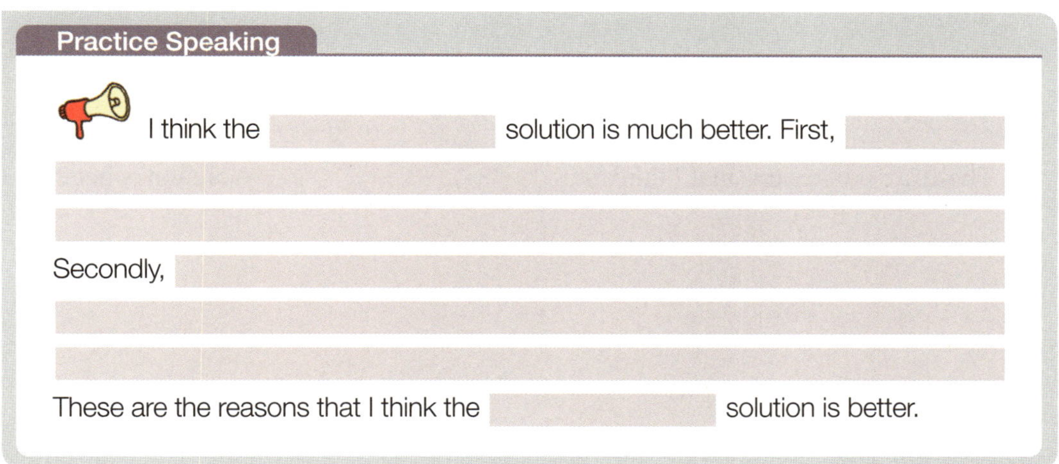

Practice Speaking

I think the ________________ solution is much better. First, ________________

Secondly, ________________

These are the reasons that I think the ________________ solution is better.

Speak Up 

The students discuss two possible solutions to the woman's problem. Describe the problem. Then state which of the two solutions you prefer and explain why.

The woman's problem is that

The man gives her   possible solutions. She could either

or she could

I think the   solution is much better.

First,

Secondly,

These are the reasons that I think the   solution is better.

09_U2_4.mp3

Listen to the sample responses and complete the notes below.

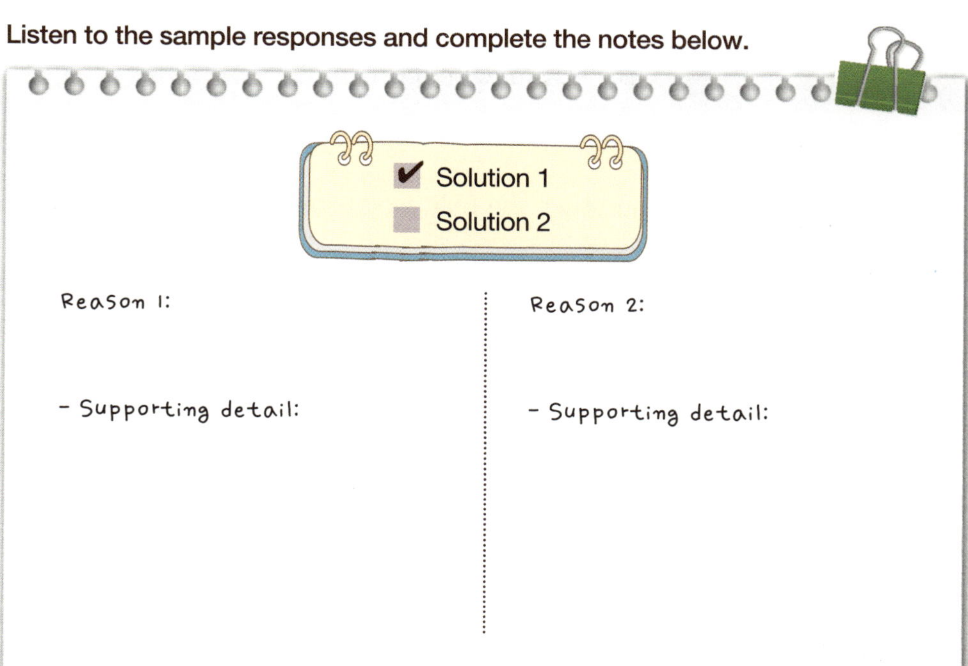

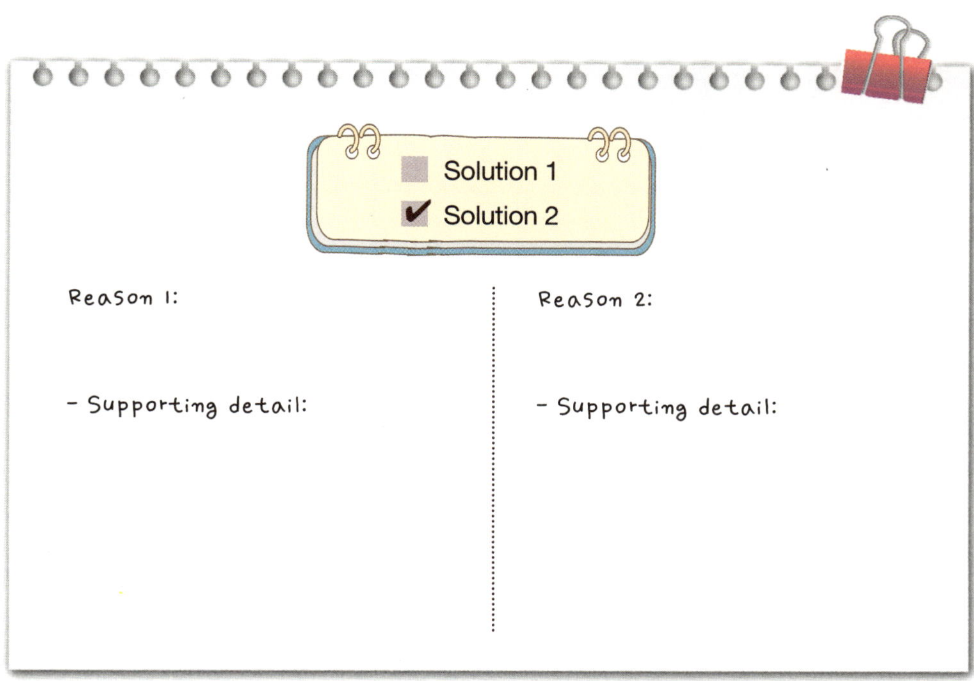

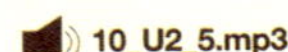

A

10_U2_5.mp3

TOEFL Speaking

PAUSE TEST | SECTION EXIT

iBT TOEFL Question

REVIEW | HELP | OK | NEXT

Listen to two students talking about the man's problem. Take notes while you are listening.

Notes

- **Man's problem:**

Solution 1:

- Detail:

Solution 2:

- Detail:

B

TOEFL Speaking

PAUSE TEST | SECTION EXIT

iBT TOEFL Question

REVIEW | HELP | OK | NEXT

The students discuss the two possible solutions to the man's problem. Describe the problem. Then state which of the two solutions you prefer and explain why.

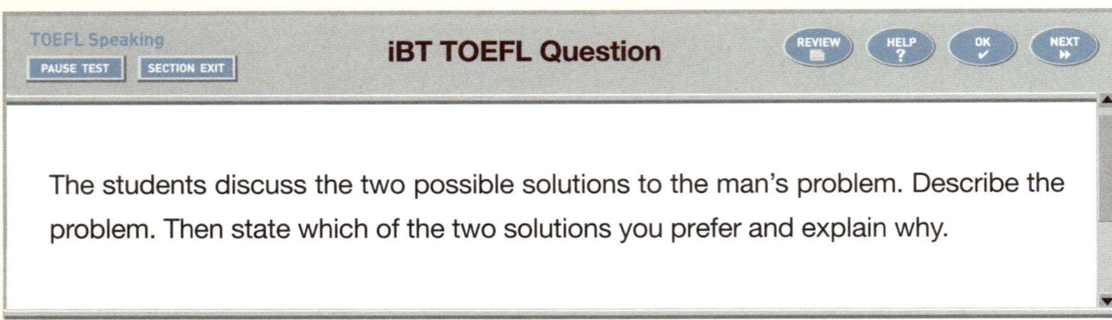

Referring to the notes in **Ⓐ**, complete the outline below for a clear response.

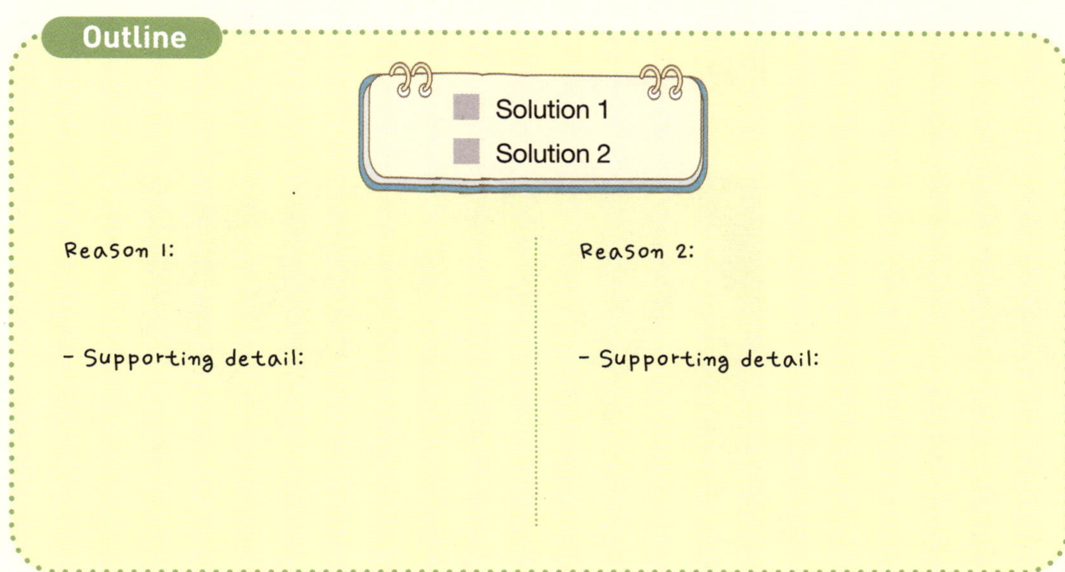

Ⓒ Referring to your outline, create your own response to the question using the key expressions below. Make sure you time while you speak.

Key Expressions

- The man's problem is that …
- The woman suggests two solutions to the problem.
- He could either … or …
- I think … is better.
- First, …
- Secondly, …
- These are the reasons that …

How long did it take for you to answer the question?

Response time:

Independent Task
Persons

•• Target iBT TOEFL Question

Independent Task

Speaking

Describe a person who is the most important to you.
Explain why the person is important to you. Include
details and examples to support your explanation.

Integrated Task
Summary

•• Target iBT TOEFL Question

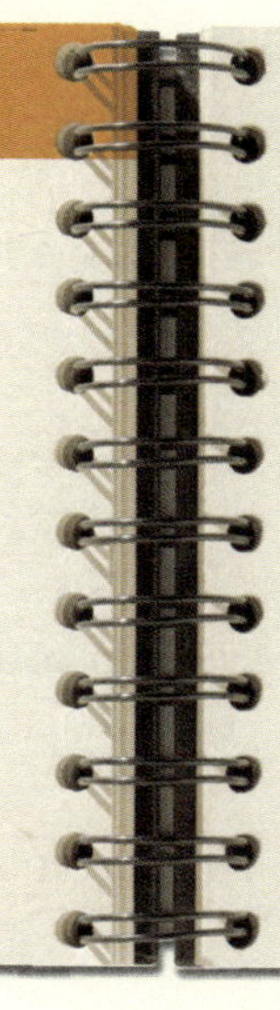

Integrated Task

Listening-Speaking

Using points and examples given in the lecture, explain two important methods that are needed when learning a new language.

Key Expressions

○ **The person who ... is ...**

e.g. The person **who is** the most important to me **is** my dad.

e.g. The person **who(m)** I admire the most **is** my English teacher.

○ **... has always p.p. ...**   (p.p. = past participle)

e.g. She **has always taken** care of me.

e.g. He **has always been** there for me.

○ **There are two reasons why ...**

e.g. **There are two reasons why** he is so important to me.

e.g. **There are two reasons why** I admire her the most.

Let's Practice

1. Who is the funniest person in your class?

   ⇨ _______________ who is the funniest in my class is _______________ .

2. Who is the most intelligent person in your class?

   ⇨ _______________ is _______________ .

3. Who do you like the most?

   ⇨ _______________ who I like the most is _______________ .

4. Who do you care about the most?

   ⇨ _______________ is _______________ .

Get Started ••

Match the words with the appropriate definitions.

① influence •   • ⓐ to get over defeat

② supportive •   • ⓑ depend on

③ overcome •   • ⓒ produce effects on actions; behavior or opinion

④ faults •   • ⓓ provide encouragement or help

⑤ rely on •   • ⓔ errors or mistakes

UNIT 3

Get Ready

Ⓐ Answer the following questions.

1 Who is the most important person to you?

⇨ The person who is the most important to me is ________________ .

2 Who is that person? (Write it down, if further information is needed about the person.)

⇨ He/She is ________________ .

Ⓑ Why do you think this person is the most important to you? Check (✔) two reasons. You may add your own answer.

☐ He/She has always been willing to help.

☐ He/She has always had an influence on me.

☐ He/She has always been supportive of me.

☐ He/She has always been patient with me.

☐ He/She has always taken care of me.

☐ ________________ .

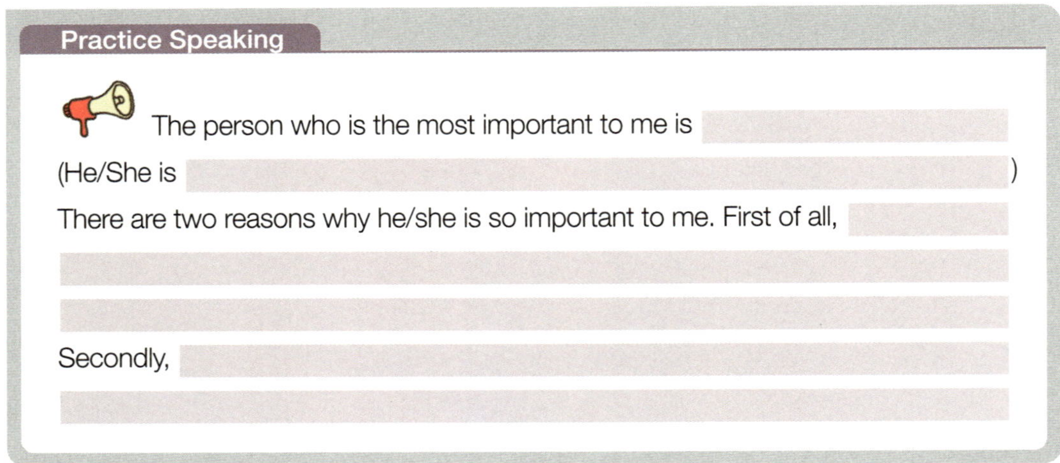

Practice Speaking

The person who is the most important to me is ________________

(He/She is ________________)

There are two reasons why he/she is so important to me. First of all, ________________

____

____

Secondly, ________________

____

C Write down the two reasons you have chosen in **B**. Then using the idea tip below as a guide, add specific details to support your two reasons. You may add your own experiences or examples to support your reasons.

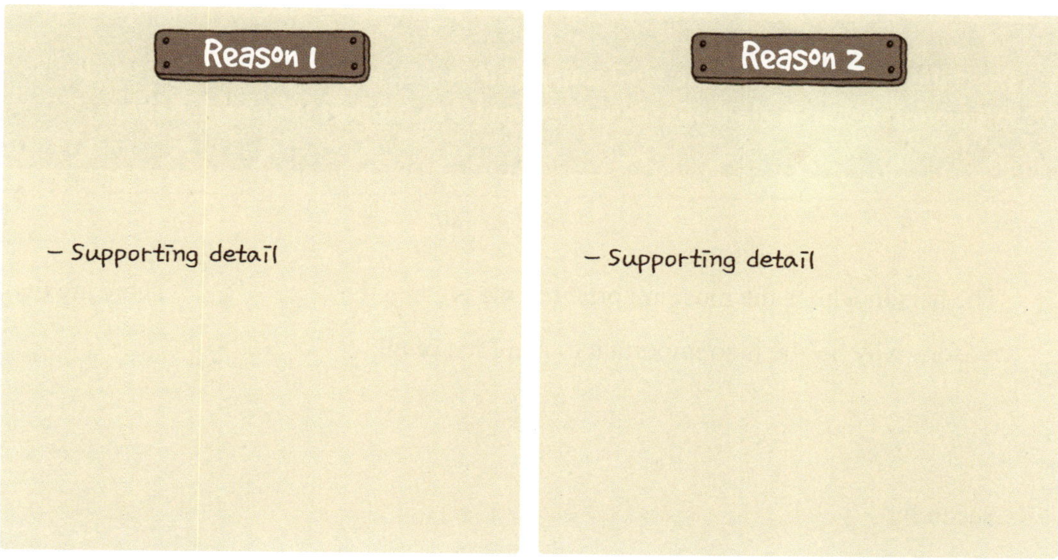

Idea Tip

- encourages me to keep trying
- leads me on the right track
- helps me overcome difficulties
- has given me the time I needed to realize my faults and fix them myself
- is always on my side
- is always there for me to rely on
- is a good listener and advisor

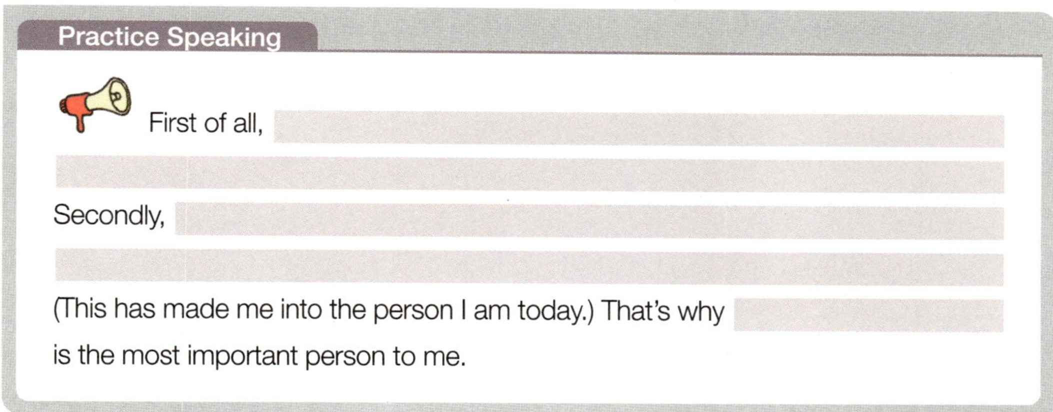

Referring from Ⓐ to Ⓒ, make your response to the question below.

> **Describe a person who is the most important to you. Explain why the person is important to you. Include details and examples to support your explanation.**

The person who is the most important to me is   There are two

reasons why he/she is so important to me. First of all,

Secondly,

(This has made me into the person I am today.) That's why

is the most important person to me.

Listen to the sample response and try to take some notes.

• **The most important person:**

Reason 1:

− Supporting detail:

Reason 2:

− Supporting detail:

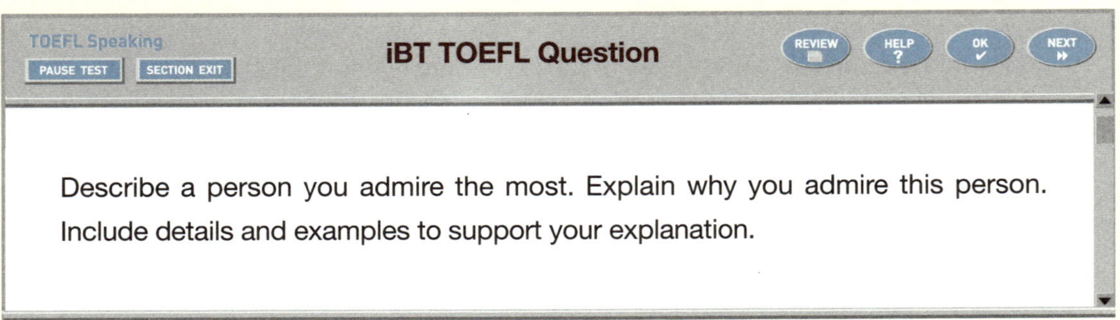

A Using the ideas below as a guide to find two major reasons, complete the outline for a response.

- He/She has sacrificed so much to provide for the family.
- He/She has become successful due to his/her own hard work.
- He/She has inspired me in a lot of ways.
- He/She has overcome his/her problems.
- He/She has have a big influence on my character.
- He/She has taught me a lot of things.

Outline

· The person I admire the most:

Reason 1:   Reason 2:

- Supporting detail: - Supporting detail:

B Referring to your outline, create your own response to the question using the key expressions below. Make sure you time while you speak.

Key Expressions

- The person who(m) I admire the most is ...
- There are two reasons why ...
- First of all, ...
- Secondly, ...
- That's why ...

How long did it take for you to answer the question?

Response time:

○ **The main topic of the lecture is …**

> **e.g.** The main topic of the lecture is vitamin C.

○ **According to the professor, …**

> **e.g.** According to the professor, there are good and bad things about vitamin C.

○ **The example the professor gives is …**

> **e.g.** The example the professor gives is Susan who took vitamin C three times a week.

○ **The professor discusses … using the example of …**

> **e.g.** The professor discusses the overdose of vitamin C **using the example of** Ted.

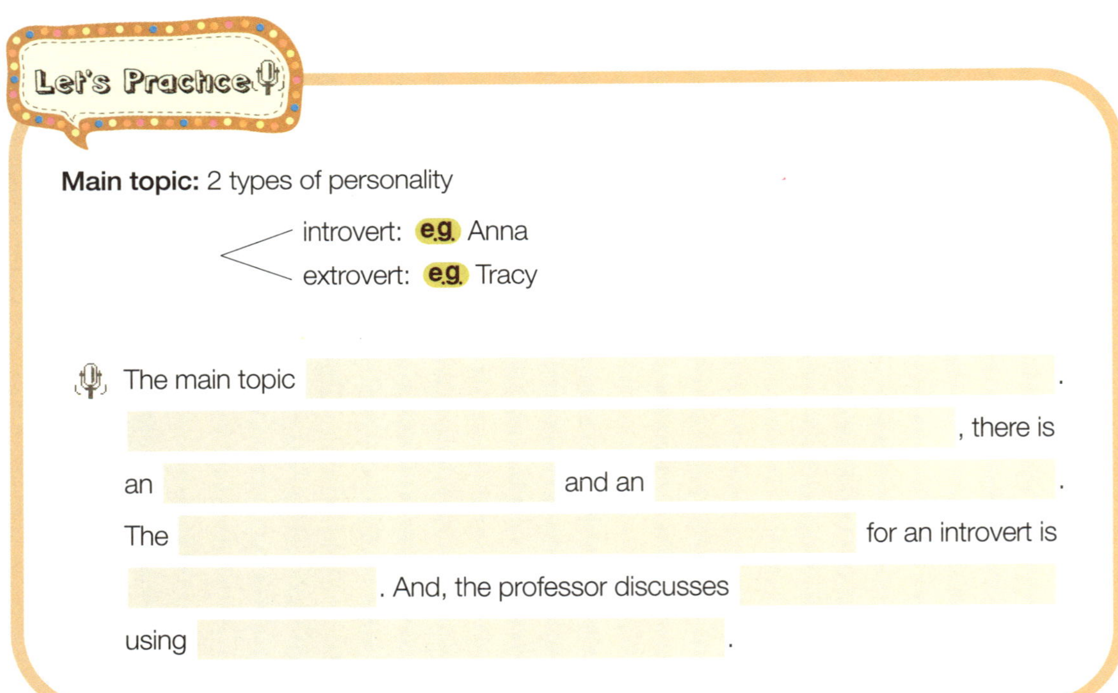

Let's Practice

Main topic: 2 types of personality

introvert: **e.g.** Anna

extrovert: **e.g.** Tracy

The main topic ____________________ .

____________________ , there is

an ____________________ and an ____________________ .

The ____________________ for an introvert is

____________________ . And, the professor discusses ____________________

using ____________________ .

Get Started ••

Match the words with the appropriate definitions.

① difficult   •   • ⓐ ways

② methods   •   • ⓑ usefully and easily

③ collect   •   • ⓒ thing, item

④ efficiently   •   • ⓓ hard

⑤ connections   •   • ⓔ gather

⑥ object   •   • ⓕ links, bonds

Get Ready ••

Ⓐ Listen to part of a lecture on learning a new language. Fill in the blanks to complete the lecture.

🔊 12_U3_2.mp3

Professor: I believe that everyone already knows that learning a new language is a very ①____________ process. When learning a new language, there are two main ②____________ that help many students learn faster. The first method is ③____________. Through repetition, people can ④____________ information faster and more ⑤____________. An example of this is when students use ⑥____________ to learn new vocabulary. Through the repetition of seeing the same word and defining it ⑦____ and ⑧____, they build a clear ⑨____ between their ⑩____ and ⑪____ to help ⑫____ new words. The second method in learning a new language is to use all five ⑬____. When something is being used through all five senses, they are making multiple ⑭____________ with the ⑮____________, ⑯____________, and the ⑰____________. An example can be seen in the word *pomme*, which means ⑱____________ in French. To learn this word, an apple must now be referred to as a *pomme*. They must now ⑲____________ the word, ⑳____________ the word, ㉑____________ the word, ㉒____________ the object, and ㉓____________ the object in order to remember *pomme*.

 Listen to the lecture again. Without looking at Ⓐ , fill in the blanks to complete the notes.

🔊 13_U3_3.mp3

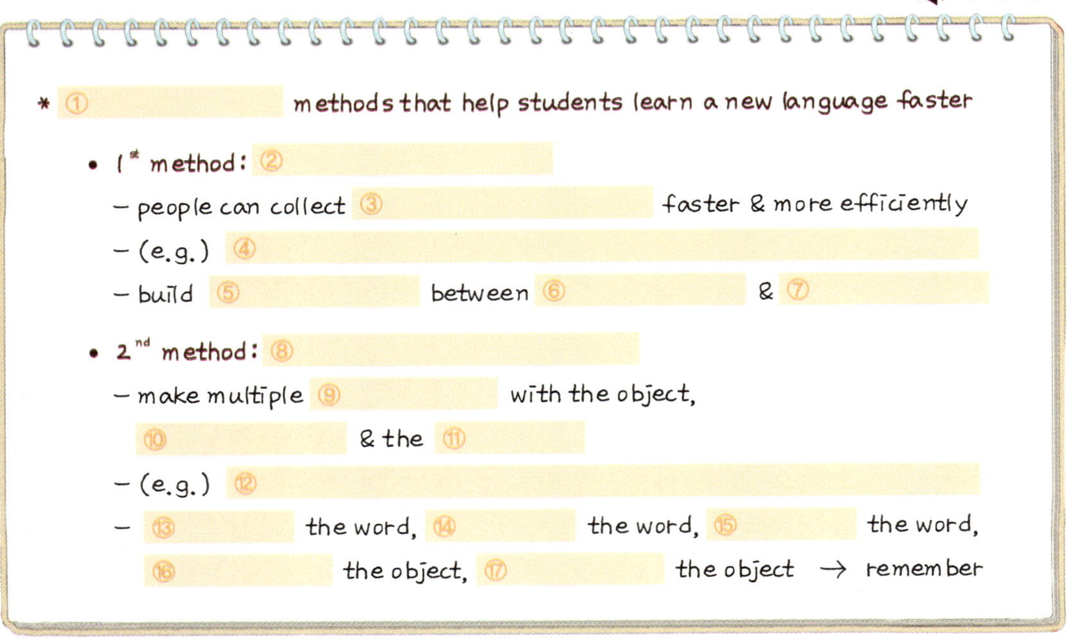

Ⓒ **Check (✔) whether the following statements are true or false.**

		True	False
1	The professor mentions that learning a new language is an easy task.	☐	☐
2	This lecture is mainly about learning new vocabulary.	☐	☐
3	The example the professor gives to explain repetition is using flashcards to help students to learn language.	☐	☐
4	Repetition does not really help to build a clear link between the eyes and the brain.	☐	☐
5	The example the professor gives to explain the usage of the five senses is the word *pomme*, the French word for apple.	☐	☐
6	By using all five senses, students are able to make connections with the object, language, and the brain.	☐	☐

D Referring to **C**, answer the following questions and practice speaking.

1 What is the main topic of the lecture?

➡ The main topic of the lecture is   .

2 According to the professor, what are the two main methods for learning a new language?

➡ According to the professor, there are   main methods for learning a new language;   and the use of all   .

3 What does the professor give as an example of repetition?

➡ The example the professor gives is students who use   to learn new   .

4 What happens when the teacher repeats the action of using flashcards?

➡ By repeating the action of using flashcards, students can build   and the brain.

5 What does the professor give as an example of using all five senses?

➡ The example the professor gives is the word   , the French word for   .

6 What happens when students use all five senses to study a new word?

➡ By using all five senses, students are able to   .

Referring from Ⓐ to Ⓓ, make your response to the question below.

Using the points and examples given in the lecture, explain two important methods that are needed when learning a new language.

The main topic of the lecture is

According to the professor,

:

and

The professor discusses the first method in learning a new language which is

The example she gives is

By repeating the action of using flashcards,

Then the professor talks about the second method which is

The example she gives is   , the french word for

By using all five senses,

Check Your Response

14_U3_4.mp3

Listen to the sample response and take notes if necessary.

UNIT 3

A   15_U3_5.mp3

Listen to the part of the lecture on peer pressure. Take notes while you are listening.

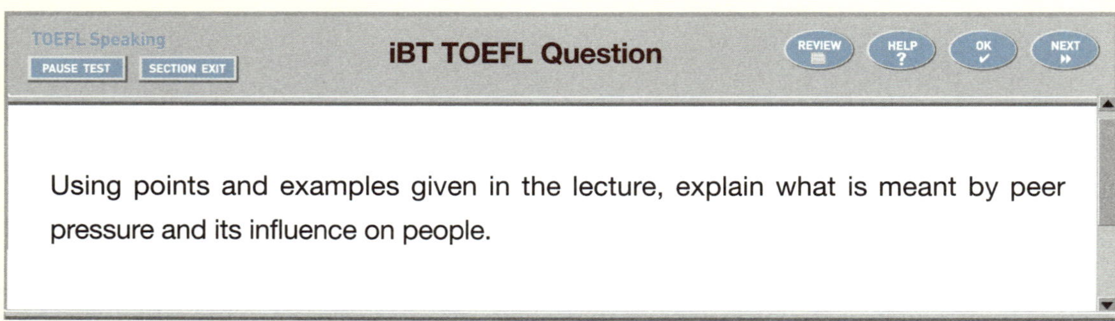

B

Using points and examples given in the lecture, explain what is meant by peer pressure and its influence on people.

Referring to the notes in **Ⓐ**, complete the outline below for a clear response.

• Peer pressure:

Negative peer pressure:

– (e.g.)

–

–

Positive peer pressure:

– (e.g.)

–

–

Ⓒ Referring to your outline, create your own response to the question using the key expressions below. Make sure you time while you speak.

- The main topic of the lecture is ...
- The professor explains that ...
- According to him, there are two types of peer pressure: ...
- The professor discusses ... using the example of ...
- Then the professor talks about ... using the example of ...

How long did it take for you to answer the question?

Response time:

Independent Task
Characteristics

•• Target iBT TOEFL Question

Independent Task

Speaking

What are the important characteristics of a student leader?
Explain why these characteristics are important.
Include details and examples to support your explanation.

Integrated Task
Summary

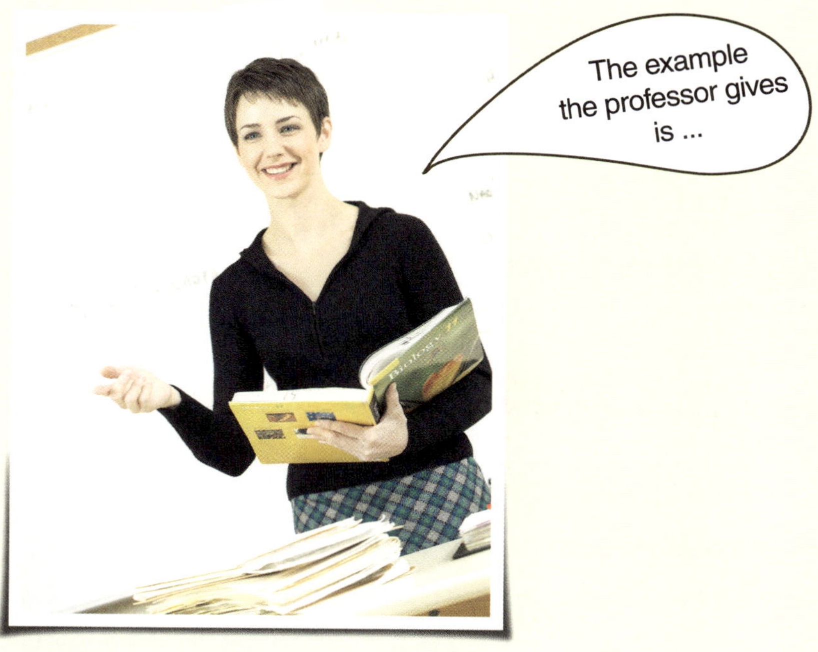

•• Target iBT TOEFL Question

Integrated Task

Listening-Speaking

Using points and examples given in the lecture, explain two methods of tools used by animals.

Key Expressions

As far as I'm concerned, ...

> **e.g.** As far as I'm concerned, there are two characteristics of a good friend.

> **e.g.** As far as I'm concerned, it's a piece of cake to solve this problem.

In my opinion, ...

> **e.g.** In my opinion, a student should have respect for his/her teacher.

> **e.g.** In my opinion, the next question is not too difficult.

should / must

> **e.g.** Students **should / must** keep quiet while the teacher explains something.

be able to

> **e.g.** Students should **be able to** concentrate for at least an hour.

> **e.g.** Every student must **be able to** solve these questions.

Let's Practice

- Learning other languages is difficult.
- English, especially, is the most difficult language to study.
- keep reading books and listening to the news / practice speaking English frequently
- improve my ability to speak English

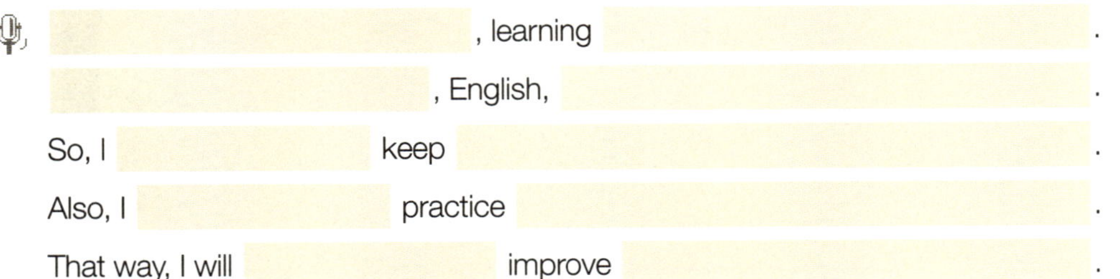

______________________ , learning ______________________ .

______________________ , English, ______________________ .

So, I ______________ keep ______________________ .

Also, I ______________ practice ______________________ .

That way, I will ______________ improve ______________________ .

Get Started

Match the words on the left with the synonyms on the right.

① impartiality

② confident

③ appeal

④ passionate

⑤ diligently

⑥ intermediary

ⓐ attractiveness

ⓑ hard; earnestly

ⓒ fairness

ⓓ agent

ⓔ certain; assured

ⓕ enthusiastic; excited

Get Ready

🅐 Answer the following questions.

1 Who is a student leader in your school now?

2 Do you think he/she is a good student leader?

▨ Yes　　　　　　　▨ No

3 What characteristics of a leader does he/she possess? Check(✔) all of them.

▨ responsibility　　▨ impartiality　　▨ passion　　▨ diligence

▨ confidence　　　▨ cleverness　　▨ open-minded

▨ good-looking　　▨ honesty　　　▨ good communication skills

B What do you think are the most important characteristics of a student leader? Check (✔) two characteristics that you think are the most important. You may add your own answer.

- A student leader should be confident about his/her own abilities.
- He/She must lead by example.
- He/She should treat other students the same.
- He/She should be responsible for other students.
- He/She must be good at communicating with other students.
- He/She must be clever.
- His/Her appearance should appeal to others.
- He/She must be honest with others.
- He/She should be passionate about his/her work.
-

Practice Speaking

As far as I'm concerned, there are two characteristics of a student leader.

In my opinion, a student leader

Also,

C Write down the two reasons you have chosen in B. Then using the idea tip below as a guide, add specific details to support your two reasons. You may add your own experiences or examples to support your reasons.

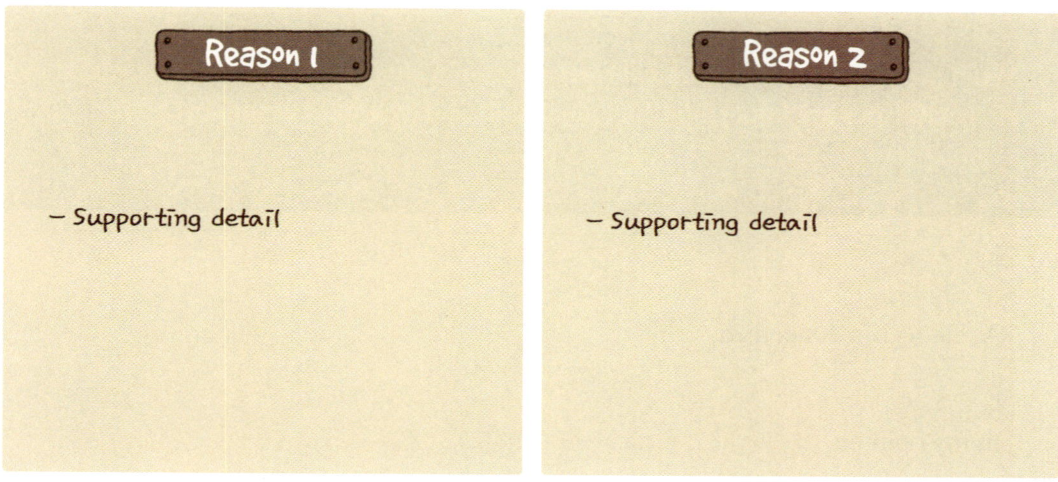

Idea Tip

- have the same beliefs
- be able to act diligently and work harder than everyone else
- be able to gain the respect of other students
- good at school studies and always on top
- popular among students
- keep his/her promises
- always ready to listen to other students' problems
- be a good intermediary between students and teachers

Practice Speaking

Speak Up

Referring from Ⓐ to Ⓒ, make your response to the question below.

> What are the most important characteristics of a student leader? Explain why these characteristics are important. Include details and examples to support your explanation.

As far as I'm concerned,

In my opinion,

Also,

Check Your Response

16_U4_1.mp3

Listen to the sample response and try to take some notes.

- Two important characteristics of a student leader:

characteristic 1:

- Supporting detail:

characteristic 2:

- Supporting detail:

UNIT 4

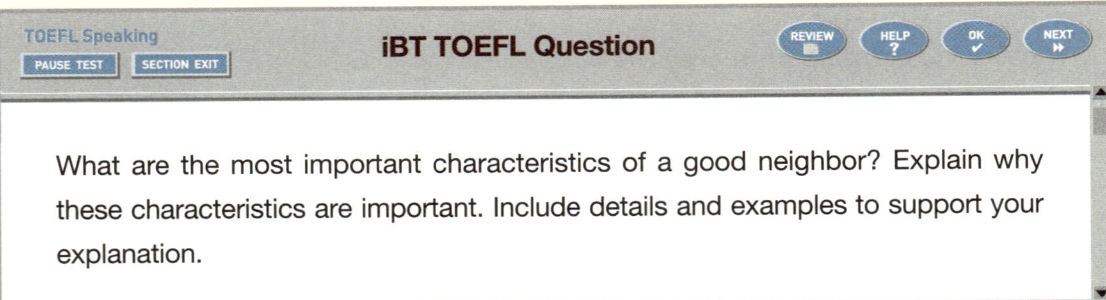

What are the most important characteristics of a good neighbor? Explain why these characteristics are important. Include details and examples to support your explanation.

A Using the ideas below as a guide to find two major reasons, complete the outline for a response.

- Neighbors should be respectful.
- Neighbors should be understanding.
- Neighbors should be friendly and nice.
- Neighbors should be honest.
- Neighbors should help each other during hard times.
- Neighbors should keep their nose out of each other's business.
- Neighbors should be quiet and tidy.

Outline

- Two important characteristics of a good neighbor:

  Characteristic 1:

  Characteristic 2:

  - Supporting detail:

  - Supporting detail:

B Referring to your outline, create your own response to the question using the key expressions below. Make sure you time while you speak.

- As far as I'm concerned, there are two important characteristics of ...
- In my opinion, ...
- Also, ...

How long did it take for you to answer the question?

Response time:

Integrated Task - Summary

- **The lecture is mainly about ...**

  e.g. The lecture is mainly about vitamin C.

- **The professor explains that ...**

  e.g. The professor explains that there are good and bad things about vitamin C.

- **The professor begins by ...**

  e.g. The professor begins by discussing some advantages of taking vitamins everyday.

- **The professor uses ... as an example.**

  e.g. The professor uses Ted who overdoses vitamin C as an example.

Let's Practice

Main point: taking a nap

　　　advantages to taking a nap　**e.g.** Ally - 20 minutes

　　　disadvantages to taking a nap

The lecture is ____.

The professor ____

______________________________________. The professor _______________

discussing some beneficial factors when taking a nap for a short time. _______

______________________________________ who sleeps for 20 minutes

after lunch ________________________________.

Get Started

Choose the word from the box that best completes the sentence.

> • solve • measure • depth • complicated • take off • fit into

1 This truck does not ________ this parking space.

2 The question I wrote on the board is very ________.

3 If anyone ________s this question, I will buy lunch.

4 The ________ of this river is about 1 foot.

5 Rulers are used to ________ things.

6 Please ________ your shoes when you enter my house.

Get Ready

A Listen to part of a lecture on animals' use of tools. Fill in the blanks to complete the lecture.

))) 17_U4_2.mp3

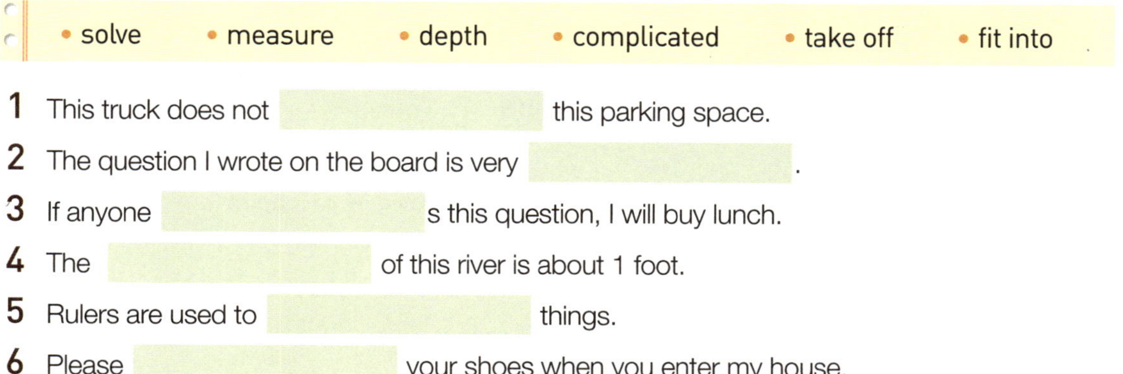

Professor: Did you know that animals are able to ① ________ the use of ② ________ to everyday activities? This shows that animals have an advanced ③ ________ to ④ ________ problems. There are two different ways animals use tools: ⑤ ________ ways and ⑥ ________ ways . The simple use of tools is when animals use ⑦ ________ or things in ⑧ ________ in their ⑨ ________ form. An example of the simple tool use comes from ⑩ ________ . Gorillas use ⑪ ________ and other long objects in nature to ⑫ ________ the ⑬ ________ of ⑭ ________ . Then what is the systematic tool use? This is a more ⑮ ________ technique, and it is similar to techniques used by ⑯ ________ . It is when a ⑰ ________ or appearance of an object is ⑱ ________ to make work ⑲ ________ . An example of this can be seen in ⑳ ________ . Chimpanzees ㉑ ________ ㉒ ________ from branches and then sharpen them with their ㉓ ________ . Chimpanzees use these sharp ㉔ ________ to ㉕ ________ into ant and termite nests. Using these tools, chimpanzees make their work more ㉖ ________ . This shows that they are more advanced in their ㉗ ________ .

◀)) 18_U4_3.mp3

* ①______ — relate the use of ②______ to everyday activities

    = have an ability to ③______ ④______

     • simple tool use: use tools in their ⑤______ form

      – (e.g.) ⑥______

      – use ⑦______ / other long ⑧______ to

       ⑨______

     • systematic tool use: ⑩______ / appearance of an object is ⑪______

      to make work easier – (e.g.) ⑫______

      – remove ⑬______ from branches → sharpen them with

       ⑭______ → use these sharp ⑮______ to fit into

       ⑯______ , termite nests

C Check (✔) whether the following statements are true or false.

                 True False

1 The lecture is mainly about the use of tools by animals.   ☐ ☐

2 Animals do not have the ability to link objects to their everyday activities.   ☐ ☐

3 Animals have problem solving abilities.   ☐ ☐

4 Some animals use tools in simple ways and some use them in systematic ways.   ☐ ☐

5 Simple tool use is when an animal uses a tool in its original form.   ☐ ☐

6 The example the professor gives to explain simple tool use is chimpanzees.   ☐ ☐

7 Systematic tool use is when the animal changes the shape of an object to serve a specific function.   ☐ ☐

8 The professor uses gorillas as an example of systematic tool use.   ☐ ☐

9 The example shows that gorillas are more clever than chimpanzees.   ☐ ☐

D Referring to **C**, answer the following questions and practice speaking.

1 What is this lecture mainly about?

⇨ The lecture is mainly about the   .

2 What does the professor explain about an animal tool use?

⇨ The professor explains that animals   .

3 What are the two techniques that animals use according to the professor?

⇨ According to the professor, some animals use tools in

and some use them in   .

4 Explain what the simple use of tools is.

⇨ Simple tool use is when the animal uses   .

5 What do gorillas use various objects such as sticks for?

⇨ They use various objects such as sticks to   .

6 Explain what the systematic use of tools is.

⇨ Systematic tool use is when the animal changes   .

7 How do chimpanzees use sticks when they want to get ants or termites?

⇨ They remove leaves from sticks and then   .

Speak Up 

Referring from Ⓐ to Ⓓ, make your response to the question below.

Using points and examples given in the lecture, explain two methods of tools used by animals.

The lecture is mainly about

The professor explains that

According to the professor,

He begins by introducing   This is

The example he gives is   They use various objects such

as sticks to

The second type of tool use he explains is

Systematic tool use is

He uses   as an example. They

◀)) 19_U4_4.mp3

Listen to the sample response and take notes if necessary.

UNIT 4

A

🔊 20_U4_5.mp3

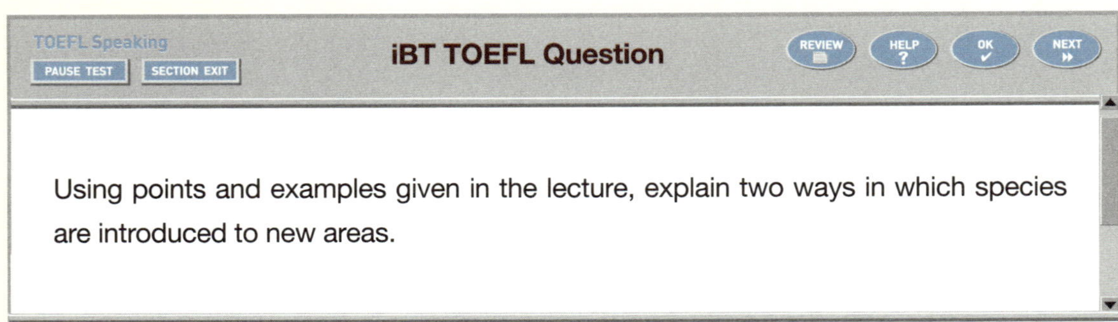

TOEFL Speaking
iBT TOEFL Question
PAUSE TEST
SECTION EXIT
REVIEW
HELP ?
OK ✔
NEXT ▸▸
Listen to the part of the lecture on introduced species. Take notes while you are listening.
Notes

B

TOEFL Speaking
iBT TOEFL Question
PAUSE TEST
SECTION EXIT
REVIEW
HELP ?
OK ✔
NEXT ▸▸
Using points and examples given in the lecture, explain two ways in which species are introduced to new areas.

Referring to the notes in Ⓐ, complete the outline below for a clear response.

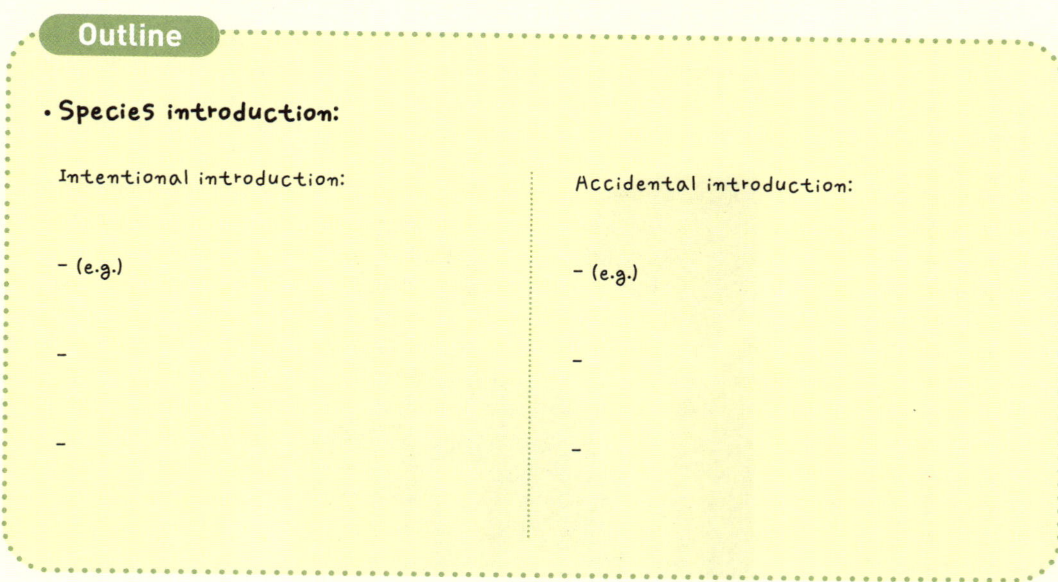

Ⓒ **Referring to your outline, create your own response to the question using the key expressions below. Make sure you time while you speak.**

How long did it take for you to answer the question?

Response time:

Independent Task
Preference

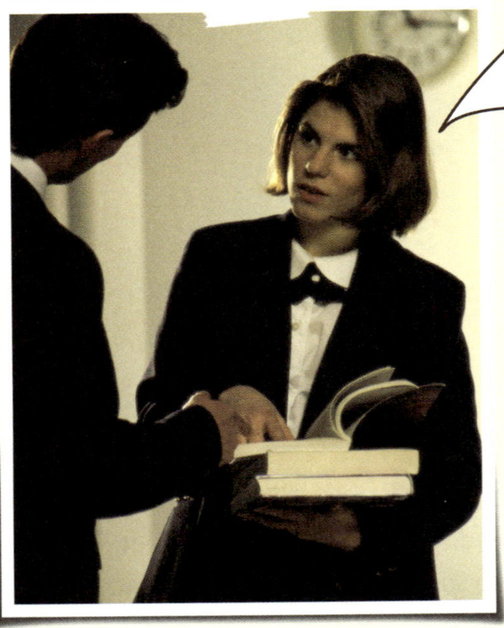

UNIT
05

•• Target iBT TOEFL Question

Independent Task

Speaking

Some students like to wear school uniforms. Others like to wear casual clothes. Which do you prefer? Explain the reasons for your opinion using details and examples.

Integrated Task
Fit & Explain

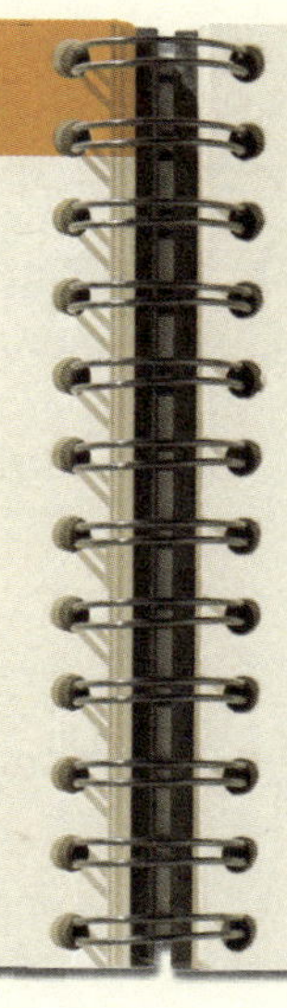

•• Target iBT TOEFL Question

Integrated Task

Reading-Listening-Speaking

The woman expresses her opinion about the notice.
State her opinion and explain the reasons she gives for
holding that opinion.

:: Independent Task - Preference

- **prefer V-ing to V-ing**   (V= Verb)

  e.g. I prefer eating at home **to eating** out.

  e.g. I prefer getting up early **to getting** up late.

- **prefer to V rather than to V**

  e.g. I prefer to eat at home **rather than to eat** out.

  e.g. I prefer to get up early **rather than to get** up late.

- **would choose to V**

  e.g. I would choose to eat at home.

  e.g. I would choose to get up early.

Let's Practice

1. I prefer studying alone to studying in a group.

   = ____ .

   = ____ .

2. I prefer to stay at home rather than to go outside on weekends.

   = ____ .

   = ____ .

Get Started

Choose the word from the box that best completes the sentence.

- rules
- comfortable
- experience
- stains
- unique

1 My teacher loved it when I came up with a ___________ idea.

2 It is good for children to learn by ___________.

3 I can't get rid of these ink ___________ on my shirt.

4 Students should obey school ___________.

5 She is a ___________ person to be with.

Get Ready

Ⓐ Answer the following questions.

1 Do you wear school uniforms?

　　　Yes (go to number 2)　　　　　No (go to number 3)

2 Do you like wearing school uniforms?

　　　Yes (go to number 4)　　　　　No (go to number 5)

3 Do you like wearing casual clothes?

　　　Yes (go to number 5)　　　　　No (go to number 2)

4 Why do you like wearing school uniforms? Choose **two** reasons.

　　　take less time to prepare every morning

　　　no need to worry about what to wear the next day

　　　don't have to spend money on shopping for clothes

　　　uniforms are a symbol of students

5 Why do you like wearing casual clothes? Choose **two** reasons.

- [ ] uniforms are ugly / casual clothes are more fashionable
- [ ] casual clothes are more comfortable
- [ ] like to look different from other people
- [ ] don't like to follow the rules much

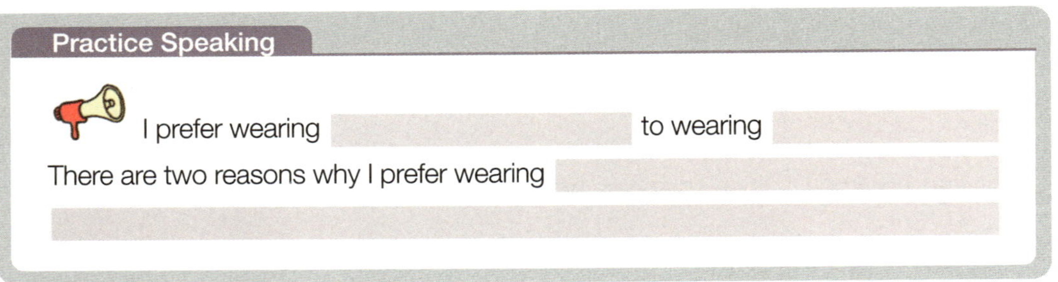

Practice Speaking

I prefer wearing ____________ to wearing ____________

There are two reasons why I prefer wearing ____________

____

B Check (✔) your preference and write down the two reasons you have chosen in **A**. Then using the idea tip as a guide, add specific details to support your two reasons.

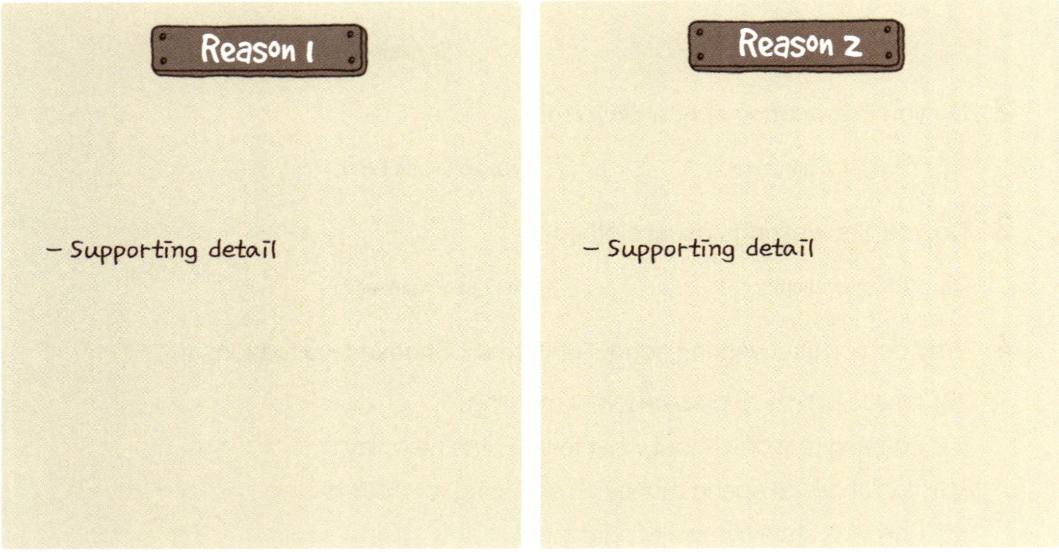

- never have to worry about what I'm going to wear
- can save money or spend money on other things, such as ...
- get to school early / late
- is a once-in-a-lifetime experience
- have my own style
- like being unique and special
- (don't) like to wear skirts and ties / more comfortable to wear jeans and t-shirts
- (don't) have to worry about wrinkles and stains

Practice Speaking

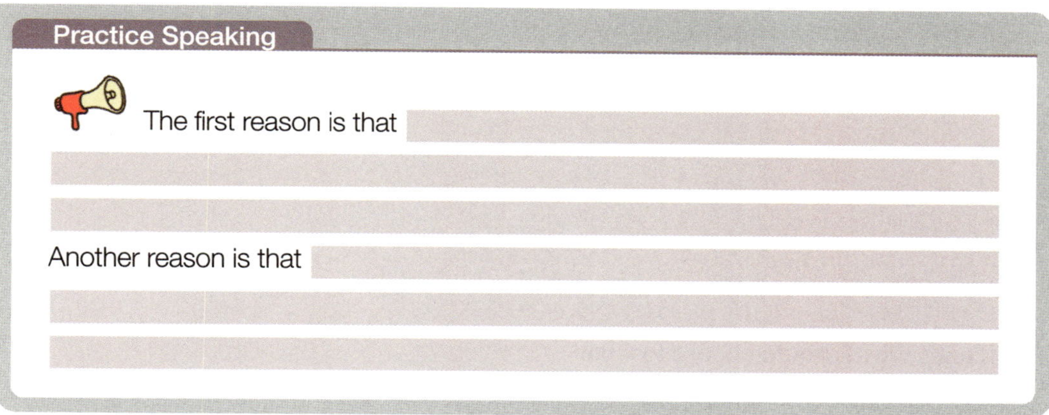

The first reason is that

Another reason is that

Speak Up

Referring from Ⓐ to Ⓑ , make your response to the question below.

Some students like to wear school uniforms. Others like to wear casual clothes.
Which do you prefer? Explain the reasons for your opinion using details and examples.

I prefer wearing   to wearing

There are two reasons why I prefer wearing

The first reason is that

Another reason is that

That's why I would choose to wear

Listen to the sample responses and complete the notes below.

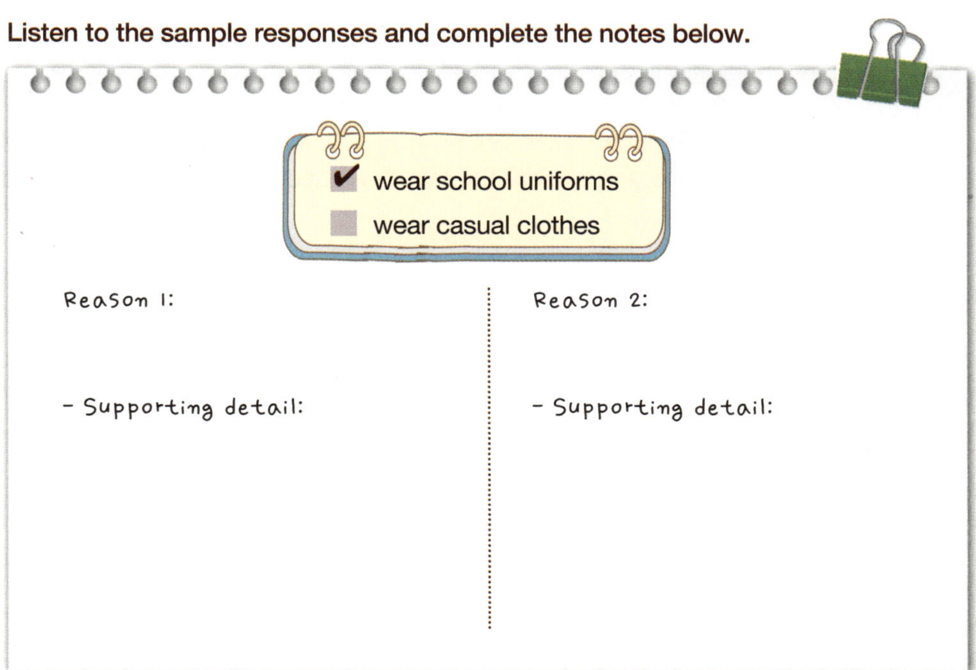

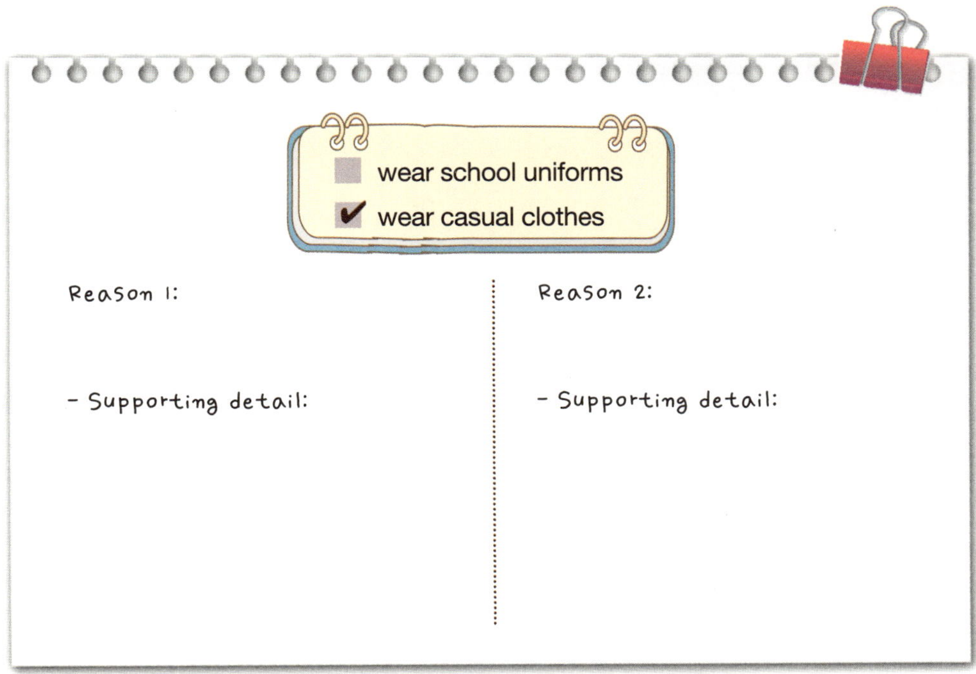

UNIT 5

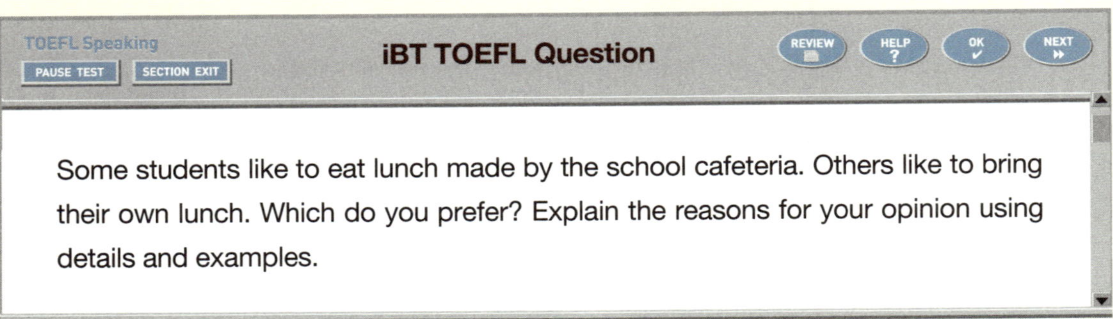

Ⓐ Using the ideas below as a guide to find two major reasons, complete the outline on the next page for a response.

☐ eat lunch made by the school cafeteria

- The food is freshly cooked.
- It is more delicious.
- I can enjoy lunch time more.
- There are always different things on the menu.

☐ bring my own lunch

- I don't have to waste time waiting in line.
- I can save money.
- It is healthier and more hygienic.
- I don't have to worry about eating too much.

■ eat lunch made by the school cafeteria
■ bring my own lunch

Reason 1:

- Supporting detail:

Reason 2:

- Supporting detail:

B Referring to your outline, create your own response to the question using the key expressions below. Make sure you time while you speak.

- I prefer to ... rather than to ...
- There are two reasons why I prefer to ...
- The first reason is that ...
- Another reason is that ...
- That's why I would choose to ...

How long did it take for you to answer the question?

Response time:

○ **... disagrees with ...**

> **e.g.** The woman **disagrees with** the university's plan.

○ **... does not agree with ...**

> **e.g.** The woman **does not agree with** the university's plan.

○ **thinks (that) ... is not a good idea**

> **e.g.** The woman **thinks (that)** the university's plan **is not a good idea.**

○ **is against N / V-ing** (N = Noun, V = Verb)

> **e.g.** The woman **is against** the university's plan.

> **e.g.** The woman **is against changing** the library's schedule.

○ **is opposed to N / V-ing** (N = Noun, V = Verb)

> **e.g.** The woman **is opposed to** the university's plan.

> **e.g.** The woman **is opposed to changing** the library's schedule.

Let's Practice

1. The man disagrees with the new proposal.

   = ____ .

   = ____ .

   = ____ .

   = ____ .

2. The man thinks raising the student union fee is not a good idea.

   = ____ .

   = ____ .

Get Started

Match the words to the right synonyms.

① renovated •

② expand •

③ facilities •

④ poor •

⑤ construction •

⑥ additional •

⑦ increase •

⑧ fair •

⑨ seniors •

• ⓐ equipment; resources

• ⓑ extra

• ⓒ remodeled; repaired

• ⓓ rise

• ⓔ enlarge; get bigger

• ⓕ reasonable

• ⓖ broken-down; bad

• ⓗ building of things

• ⓘ fourth year students in university

Get Ready

A-1 **Read the notice about the recreation center. Underline the main idea of the notice.**

Plans for Recreation Center

The Recreation Center Committee proposed to have the student recreation center renovated and its facilities expanded due to poor facilities and large numbers of students using the center. The expansion that is due to be completed by March of next year includes the construction of additional basketball courts, badminton courts and squash courts. Because this is a big project, the construction will take more time and money. Therefore, there will be a slight increase in the existing Student Union fee during the construction. However, students will be provided with a larger and more convenient recreation center.

1 What is the main idea of the notice?

Ⓐ The Recreational Center Committee is going to remodel the student recreation center.

Ⓑ The Recreational Center Committee is going to reduce the facilities of the student recreation center.

2 Why is the construction needed? Choose **two** answers.

Ⓐ because the facilities are old

Ⓑ because there is no badminton court

Ⓒ because the facilities are inadequate

3 When will the construction be done?

Ⓐ not later than March

Ⓑ after March

Ⓒ by May

4 What will the construction of this big project require? Choose **two** answers.

Ⓐ more workers

Ⓑ more time

Ⓒ more money

5 What will happen to the Student Union fee?

Ⓐ There will not be any changes to the Student Union fee.

Ⓑ The Student Union fee will rise during the building process.

Ⓒ The entrance fee will increase after the construction is done.

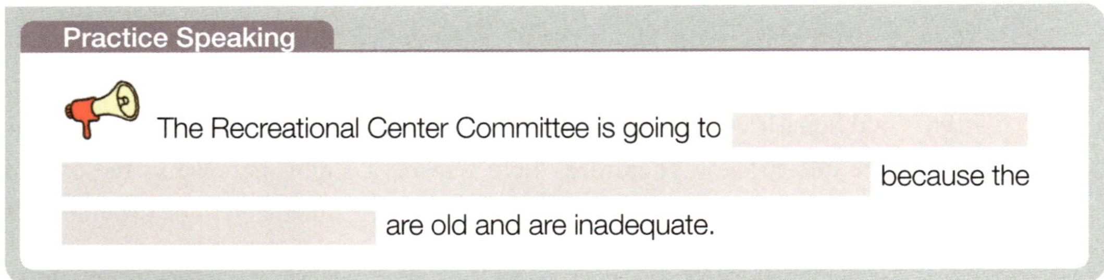

Practice Speaking

The Recreational Center Committee is going to ________________ ____ because the ________________ are old and are inadequate.

◀)) 22_U5_2.mp3

W: Did you see the ① ________ about the recreation center?

M: No. What's it about?

W: They're going to ② ________ the recreation center!

M: Well, I think it's a great idea! The basketball court we're using now is terrible. The locker rooms are particularly bad. It's about time they ③ ________ that place.

W: Do you really think so? I think it's a big waste of ④ ________ and ⑤ ________. I go to the recreation center regularly to use the fitness center and ⑥ ________ pool. I think the ⑦ ________ are excellent and I've never had to wait in ⑧ ________. They have plenty of ⑨ ________.

M: That's strange. I had to wait for at least an hour whenever I wanted to use a badminton court.

W: Well, perhaps only Fridays and ⑩ ________ are ⑪ ________. Besides, do you know that we have to ⑫ ________ for the new recreation center? We can't ⑬ ________ it much anyway, because we are graduating in ⑭ ________ next year. I don't think that's ⑮ ________ to ⑯ ________.

1 Who thinks the university's plan to renovate the student recreation center is **not** a good idea?

   Ⓐ man

   Ⓑ woman

2 What are **two** main reasons why the person disagrees with the plan?

   Ⓐ The basketball courts are fine.

   Ⓑ It is not busy Monday to Thursday.

   Ⓒ It's a big waste of time and money.

   Ⓓ It's unfair that seniors have to pay for the construction.

Practice Speaking

The woman thinks the university's plan to renovate the student recreation center is ________________ idea. There are two main reasons why she ________________ with the plan.

 Listen to the dialogue again. Without looking at **, complete the notes on the reasons why the person disagrees.**

23_U5_3.mp3

- **Reason 1:** waste of ① ______________ & ② ______________
  − Supporting detail
    : facilities are ③ ______________
    : has never had to ④ ______________ in line
    : ⑤ ______________ of space on the weekdays

- **Reason 2:** unfair that ⑥ ______________ have to pay for the construction
  − Supporting detail
    : can use the center only for ⑦ ______________ months
    : ⑧ ______________ in June next year

Practice Speaking

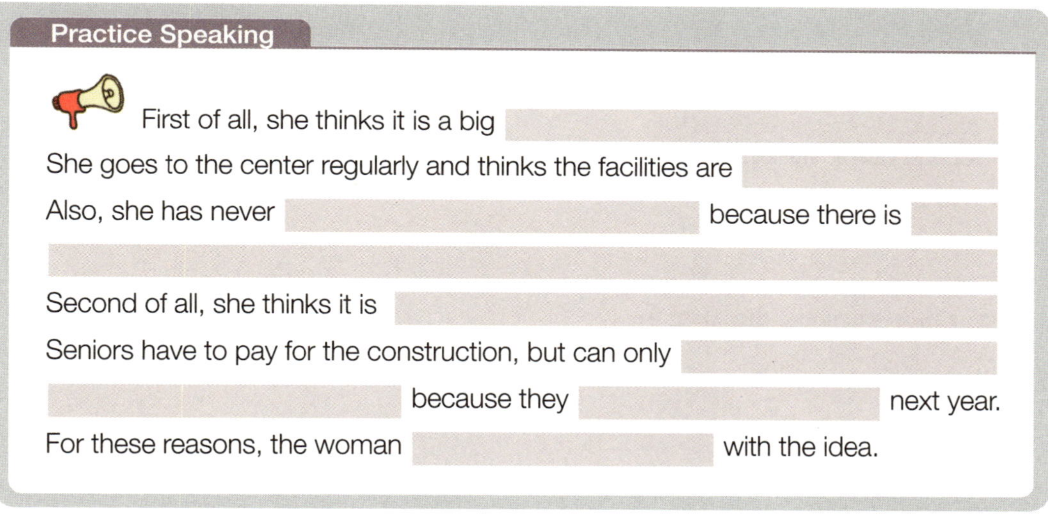

First of all, she thinks it is a big ______________
She goes to the center regularly and thinks the facilities are ______________
Also, she has never ______________ because there is ______________
____
Second of all, she thinks it is ______________
Seniors have to pay for the construction, but can only ______________
______________ because they ______________ next year.
For these reasons, the woman ______________ with the idea.

Speak Up

Referring from **Ⓐ** to **Ⓑ**, make your response to the question below.

The Recreational Center Committee is going to

because

The woman thinks the university's plan to renovate the student recreation center is

There are two main reasons why she

with the plan. First of all, she thinks

Second of all, she thinks

For these reasons, the woman   with the idea.

Listen to the sample response and take notes if necessary.

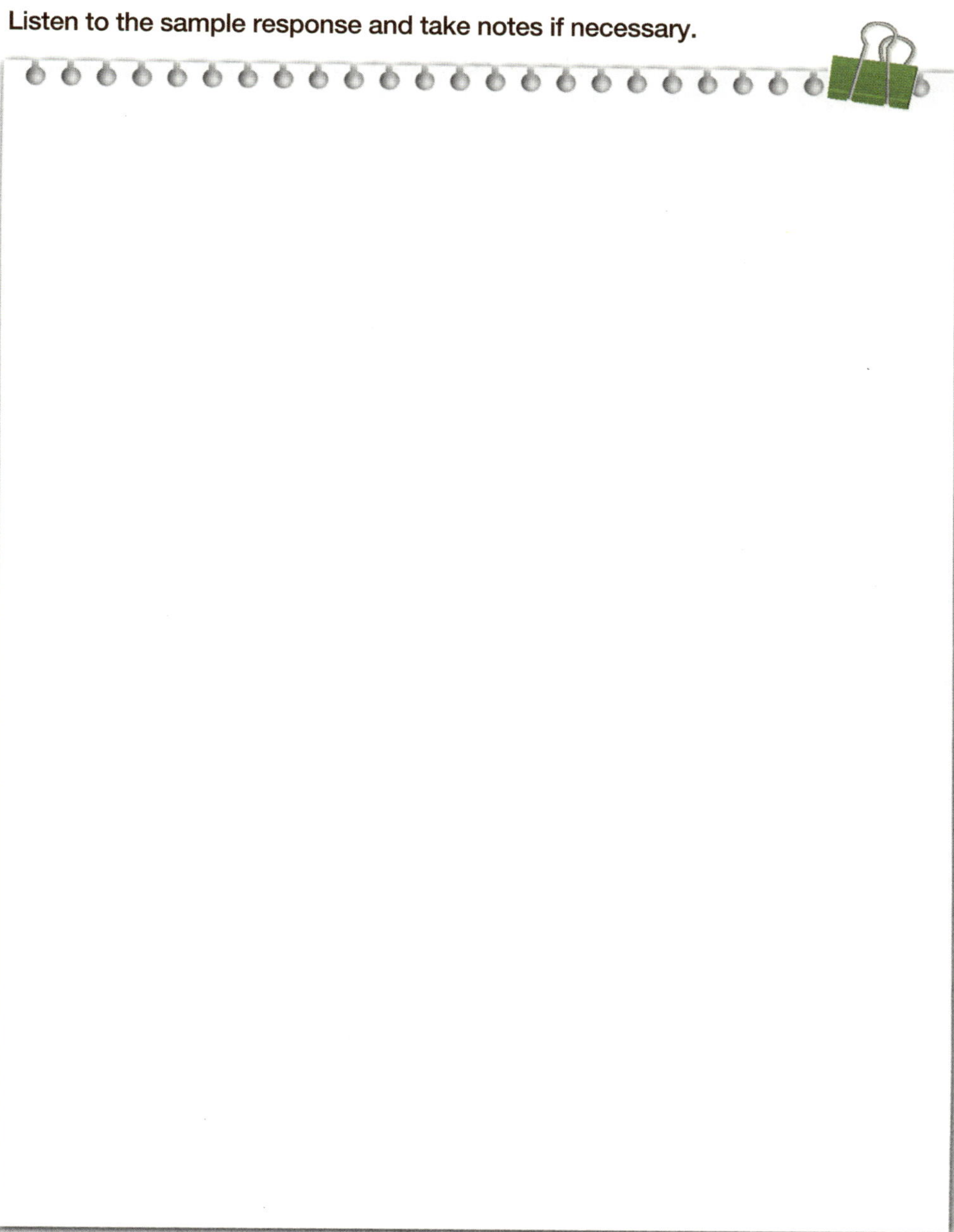

Ⓐ Read the announcement about new library hours.

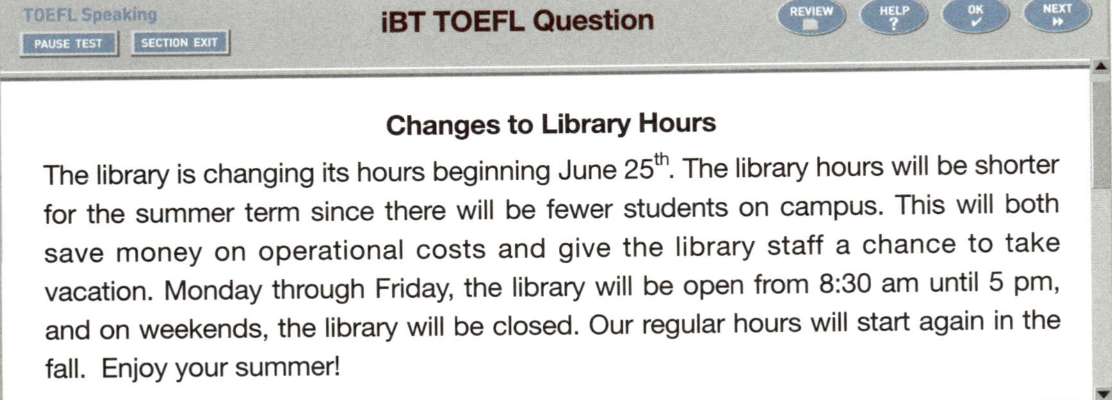

Ⓑ   🔊 25_U5_5.mp3

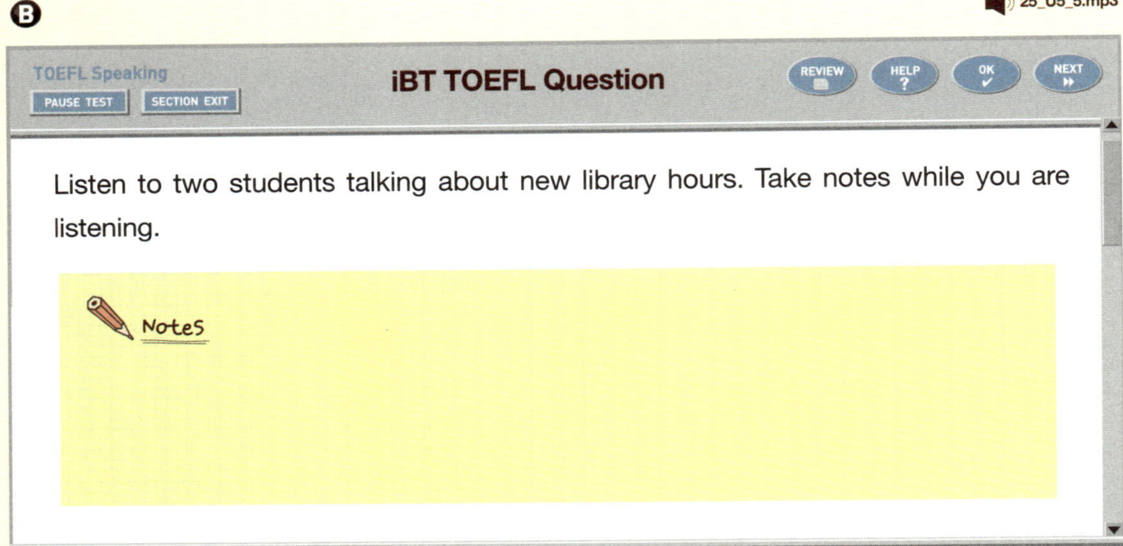

Ⓒ

Referring to **A** and **B**, complete the outline below for a clear response.

- Main idea of the announcement:

- Man's opinion:

Reason 1:

Reason 2:

– Supporting detail:

– Supporting detail:

D Referring to your outline, create your own response to the question using the key expressions below. Make sure you time while you speak.

- The library is going to ...
- The man is ...
- There are two main reasons why he thinks ...
- First of all, he thinks ...
- Second of all, he thinks ...
- For these reasons, ...

How long did it take for you to answer the question?

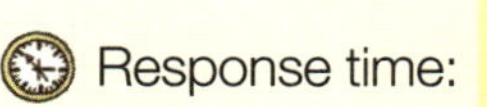 Response time:

Independent Task
Preference

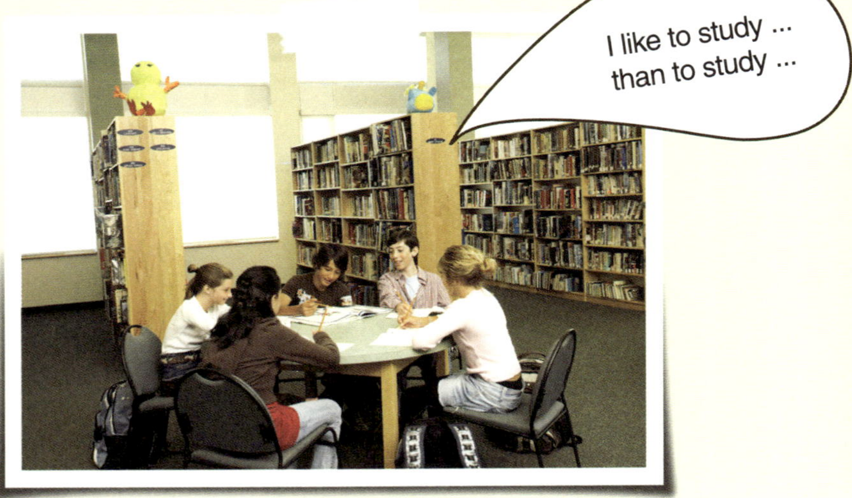

•• Target iBT TOEFL Question

Independent Task

Speaking

Some students like to study at home. Others like to study in the library. Which do you prefer? Explain the reasons for your opinion using details and examples.

Integrated Task
Fit & Explain

•• Target iBT TOEFL Question

Integrated Task

Reading-Listening-Speaking

The woman expresses her opinion about the notice.
State her opinion and explain the reasons she gives for
holding that opinion.

Independent Task - Preference

○ **like to V rather than to V**   (V = Verb)

e.g. I like to eat at home **rather than to eat** out.

e.g. I like to get up early **rather than to get** up late.

○ **would rather V than V**

e.g. I would rather eat at home **than eat** out.

e.g. I would rather get up early **than get** up late.

○ **think V-ing is better than V-ing**

e.g. I think eating at home **is better than eating** out.

e.g. I think getting up early **is better than getting** up late.

Let's Practice

1. I like to live in the countryside rather than to live in a city.

   = ____ .

   = ____ .

2. I think going to a museum is better than going to an amusement park.

   = ____ .

   = ____ .

Get Started

Choose the word from the box that best completes the sentence.

- effectively
- competitiveness
- distractions
- secluded
- provoke

1 When one of our team members injured, it increased our ______________ .

2 My grandfather lives in a ______________ mountain cottage.

3 My teacher taught me how to manage time ______________ .

4 The comedy show ______________ d laughter among my family.

5 There are too many ______________ in this room, so I can't concentrate well.

Get Ready

Ⓐ Answer the following questions.

1 Where do you usually study?

　At home (go to number 2)　　　　In the library (go to number 3)

2 Do you like to study at home?

　Yes (go to number 4)　　　　No (go to number 3)

3 Do you like to study in the library?

　Yes (go to number 5)　　　　No (go to number 2)

4 Why do you like studying at home? Choose **two** reasons.

　can study more effectively
　can save time
　have my own study style
　much more comfortable

5 Why do you like studying in the library? Choose **two** reasons.

- can concentrate deeply on my studies
- fewer distractions
- have lots of study materials to refer to
- can provoke competitiveness

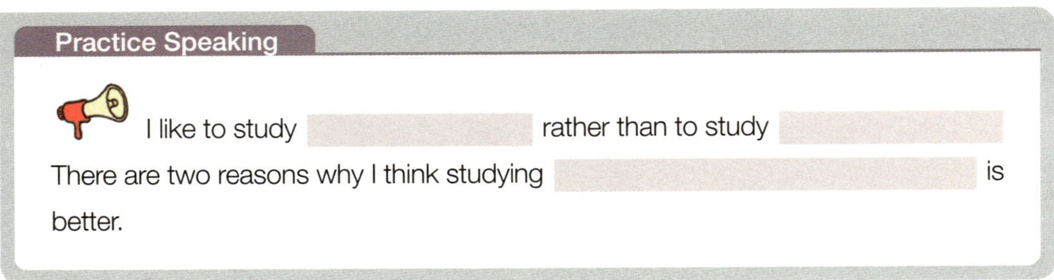

B Check (✔) your preference and write down the two reasons you have chosen in **A**. Then using the idea tip as a guide, add specific details to support your two reasons.

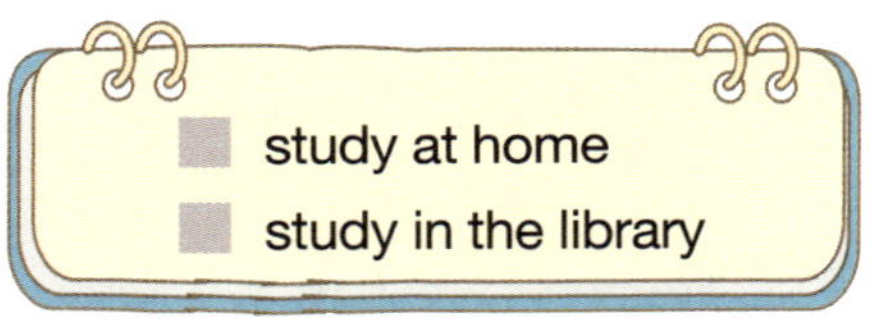

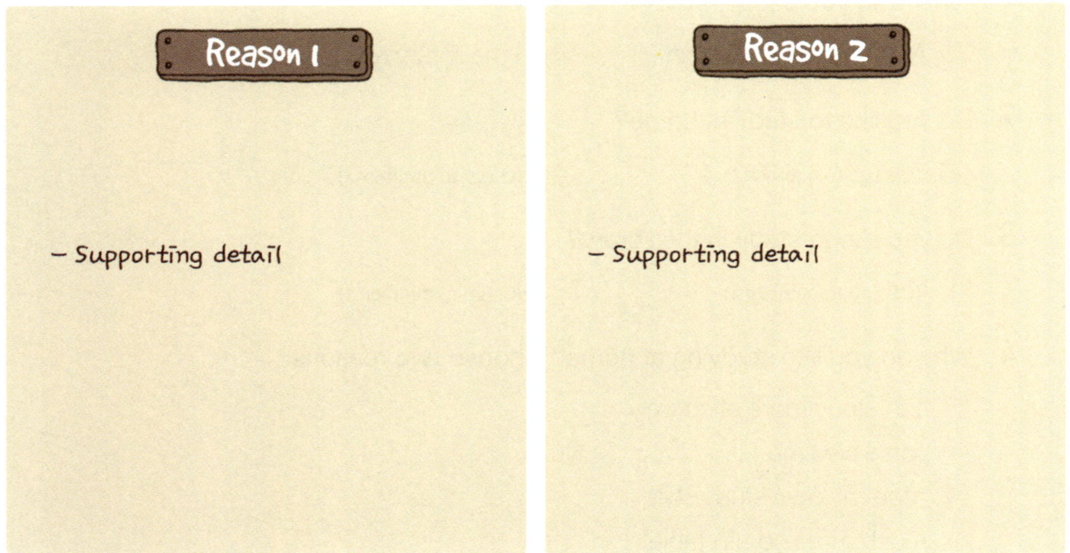

- no seating competition / too many people
- make lots of noise (e.g. people walking pass / people talking)
- turn on the T.V., go on the internet, talk on the phone with my friends, fall asleep
- concentrate better in a secluded area
- lots of pressure
- memorize things by saying them aloud repeatedly / walk around the house to clear my thoughts
- see lots of students studying very hard
- sit on my bed and study in my pajamas
- can take a break whenever I want to

Practice Speaking

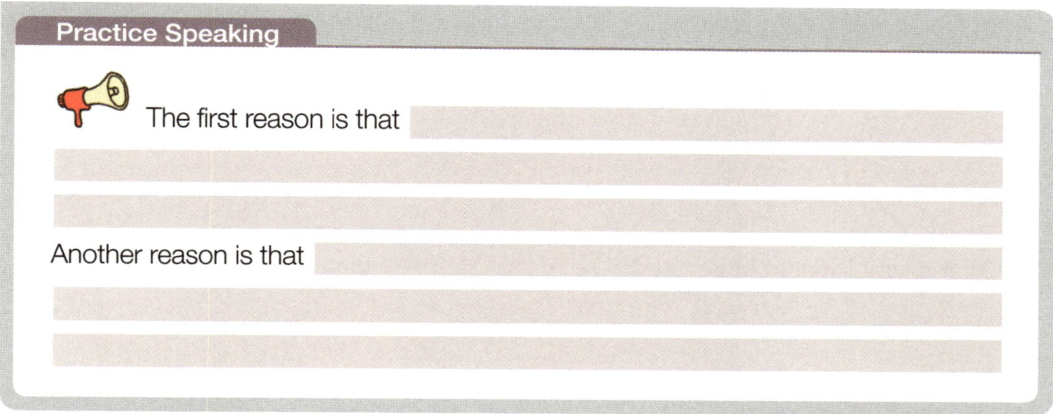

The first reason is that

Another reason is that

UNIT 6

Referring from (A) to (B), make your response to the question below.

Some students like to study at home. Others like to study in the library. Which do you prefer? Explain the reasons for your opinion using details and examples.

I like to study ____________ rather than to study ____________

There are two reasons why I think studying ____________ is better.

The first reason is that ____________

____

____

Another reason is that ____________

____

____

That's why I would rather study ____________ than study ____________

)) 26_U6_1.mp3

Listen to the sample responses and complete the notes below.

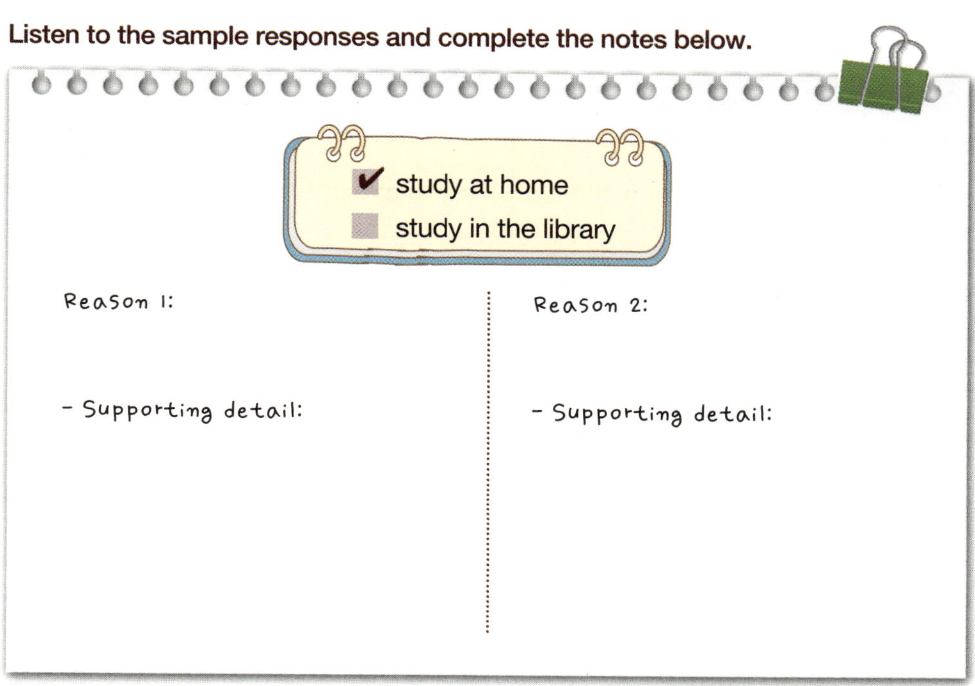

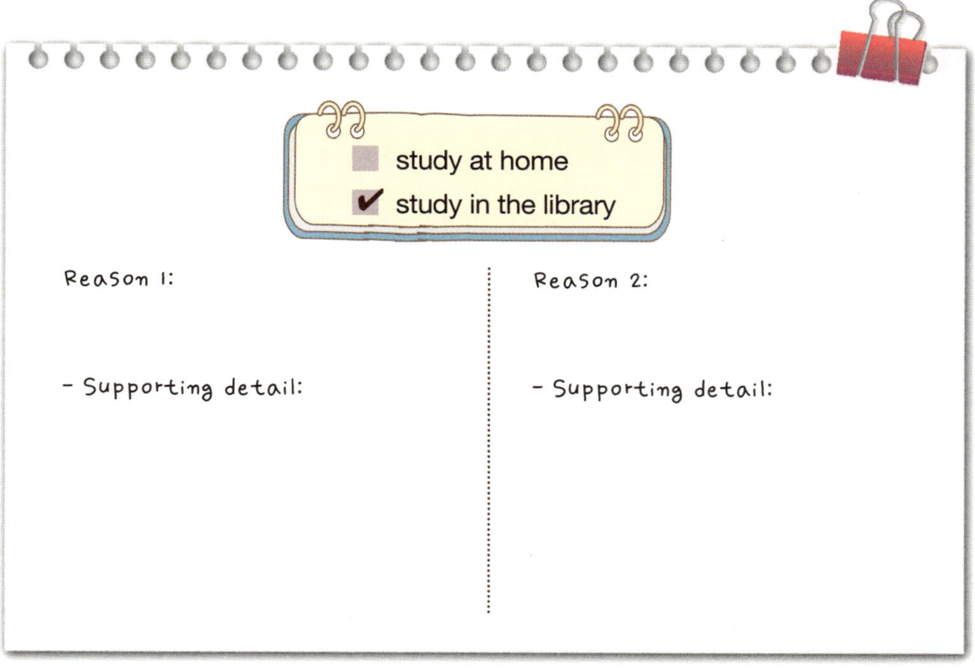

UNIT 6

TOEFL Speaking

PAUSE TEST | SECTION EXIT

iBT TOEFL Question

REVIEW | HELP ? | OK ✔ | NEXT ▶▶

Some students like to take courses on campus. Others like to take courses on-line. Which do you prefer? Explain the reasons for your opinion using details and examples.

Ⓐ Using the ideas below as a guide to find two major reasons, complete the outline on the next page for a response.

☐ take courses on campus

☐ I am not a self-motivated person.

☐ I can interact with other students.

☐ If taking courses on-line, it can be inconvenient to access the internet every day.

☐ I can understand things more easily.

☐ take courses on-line

☐ Taking courses on-line can be more convenient.

☐ It can be more flexible.

☐ I can watch lectures at any time.

☐ I can watch lectures anywhere there is an internet connection.

☐ take courses on campus
☐ take courses on-line

Reason 1:

- Supporting detail:

Reason 2:

- Supporting detail:

B Referring to your outline, create your own response to the question using the key expressions below. Make sure you time while you speak.

- I think V-ing is better than V-ing ...
- There are two reasons why I like to ...
- The first reason is that ...
- Another reason is that ...
- That's why I would choose to V ...

How long did it take for you to answer the question?

Response time:

Key Expressions

○ **... agrees with ...**

  e.g. The woman **agrees with** the university's plan.

○ **is for N**   **(N=Noun)**

  e.g. The woman **is for** the university's plan.

○ **thinks ... is a good idea**

  e.g. The woman **thinks** the university's plan **is a good idea.**

  e.g. The woman **thinks** changing the library's schedule **is a good idea.**

○ **thinks it is a good idea to V**   **(V=Verb)**

  e.g. The woman **thinks it is a good idea to change** the library's schedule.

Let's Practice

1. The man agrees with the new proposal.

  = ____ .

  = ____ .

2. The man thinks raising the student union fee is a good idea.

  = ____ .

Get Started

Answer the following questions.

1 What is a similar word for **restrictions**?

  Ⓐ rules   Ⓑ policies   Ⓒ limits

2 What is the opposite word for **seniors**?

  Ⓐ sophomore   Ⓑ freshmen   Ⓒ old students

3 What is a similar word for **privileges**?

  Ⓐ special exceptions   Ⓑ prestige   Ⓒ prize

4 What is the meaning of **malfunction**?

  Ⓐ work well   Ⓑ need repairs   Ⓒ break down

5 What is a synonym for **crowded**?

  Ⓐ full   Ⓑ empty   Ⓒ noisy

Get Ready

A-1 Read the notice about changes to printing policy. Underline the main idea of the notice.

Changes to Printing Policy

Since students have to wait a long time for their turn to print, there will now be restrictions on the usage of paper for the printers in the computer lab. The restrictions will be based on students' class year, and this policy will only apply during the exam period. Students can now check the number of pages available to them on the school website by logging in to their accounts. Seniors will be given special exceptions due to their status. We apologize for any inconvenience during the exam period.

1 What is the main idea of the notice?

   Ⓐ The university plans to restrict the usage of the computer lab based on class year.

   Ⓑ The university plans to limit the maximum amount of printing based on the student's year of study.

2 When will this printing policy apply?

   Ⓐ during the semester

   Ⓑ during the exam period

3 How can students check the number of pages they can print out?

   Ⓐ on the school website by logging in to their accounts

   Ⓑ on the printing card

4 Who is the exception to this policy?

   Ⓐ seniors

   Ⓑ freshmen

Practice Speaking

The university plans to ______________________________

based on ______________________________

🔊 27_U6_2.mp3

M: Hey, did you happen to see the notice about printing paper in the computer lab?

W: Yes, I did. You seem quite ① ________ about it. It's only for the ② ________ period, isn't it?

M: I just think it's unfair for ③ ________ . I think we should have the same right as the seniors.

W: Yes, but it's true that ④ ________ have a lot more to print than us. They have to print more because they have to write longer essays. It makes sense that they should get the ⑤ ________ .

M: Well, I usually print out my lecture notes to help me study, but now we have to ⑥ ________ for it at some internet cafés or ⑦ ________ . That is going to be so expensive.

W: Yes, but internet cafés and libraries are ⑧ ________ crowded. The computer lab may have been free, but do you remember what happened last exam period?

M: No. What happened?

W: It was so ⑨ ________ ! The printers began to ⑩ ________ and you had to ⑪ ________ at least 30 minutes just to print a few pages. Plus, I remember one time when the printers ⑫ ________ down and I had to wait in ⑬ ________ for 20 minutes. I didn't get to print anything!

M: Yeah, I do remember that. I guess it's just that I'm used to it being free.

W: It's not too ⑭ ________ . I'd rather pay the extra 50 cents.

1 Who is for the university's plan?

    Ⓐ man

    Ⓑ woman

2 What are **two** main reasons why the person agrees with the changes?

    Ⓐ The person thinks freshmen do not have anything to print.

    Ⓑ The person understands that seniors have a heavier workload than freshmen.

    Ⓒ The computer lab is always crowded and its printers often break down.

    Ⓓ The person thinks that printers in the computer lab are so old.

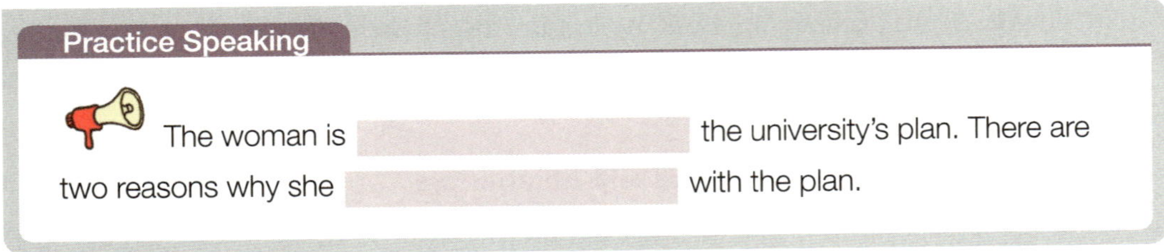

Practice Speaking

The woman is ____________ the university's plan. There are two reasons why she ____________ with the plan.

 Listen to the dialogue again. Without looking at **B-1**, complete the notes on the reasons why the person agrees.

◀)) 28_U6_3.mp3

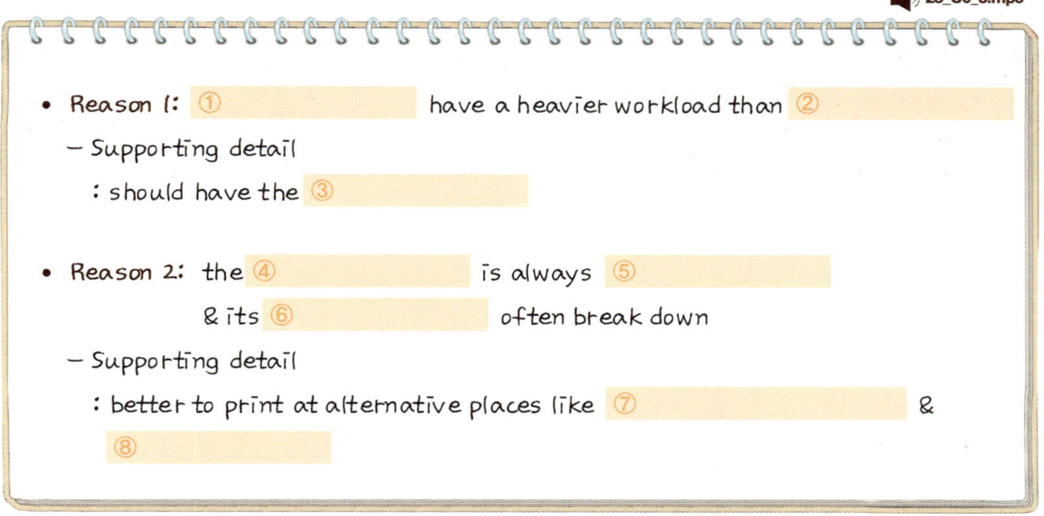

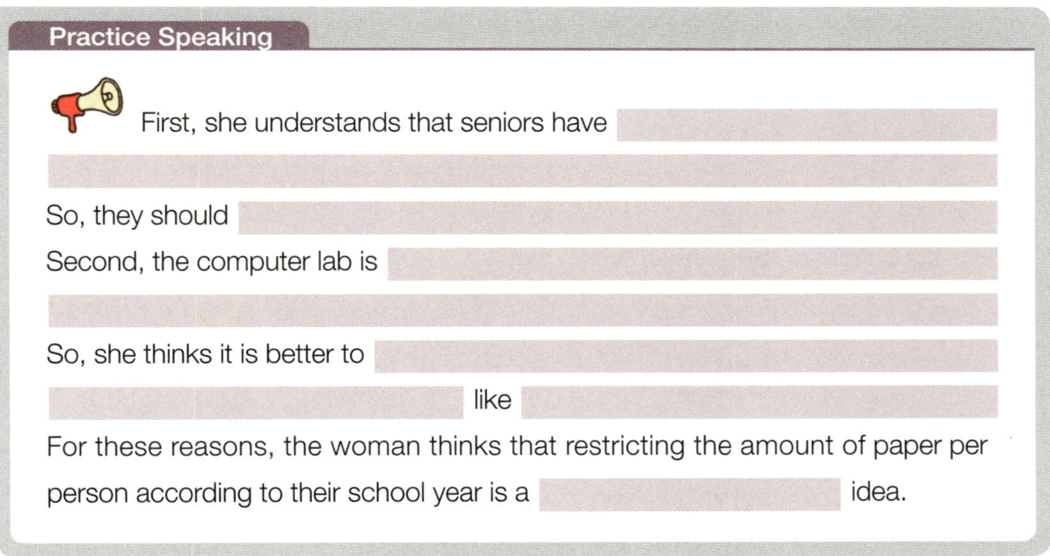

Practice Speaking

UNIT 6

Speak Up 

Referring from Ⓐ to Ⓑ, make your response to the question below.

The woman expresses her opinion about the notice. State her opinion and explain the reasons she gives for holding that opinion.

The university plans to

The woman is   the university's plan. There are two reasons why she

                          with the plan. First,

So, they should

Second,

So, she thinks it is better to

For these reasons, the woman thinks that

Check Your Response

29_U6_4.mp3

Listen to the sample response and take notes if necessary.

UNIT 6

A Read the announcement about cutting the music program.

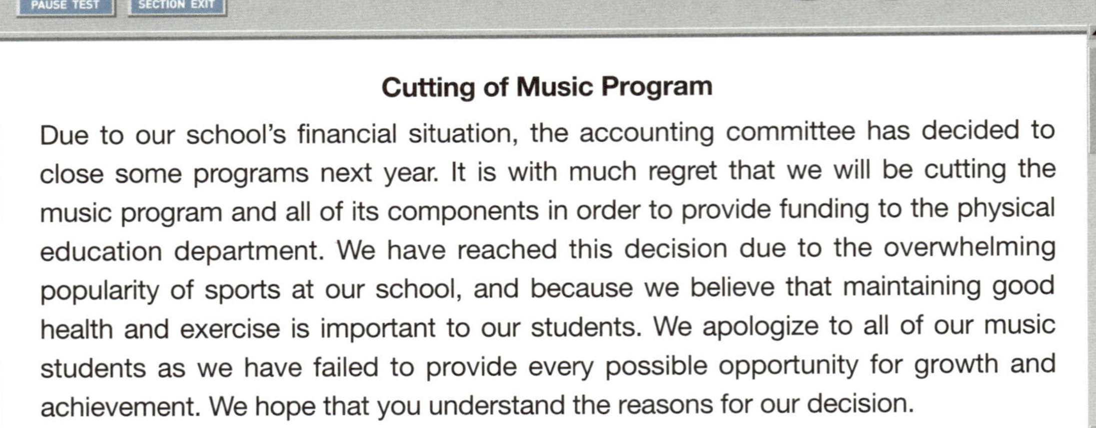

B

🔊 30_U6_5.mp3

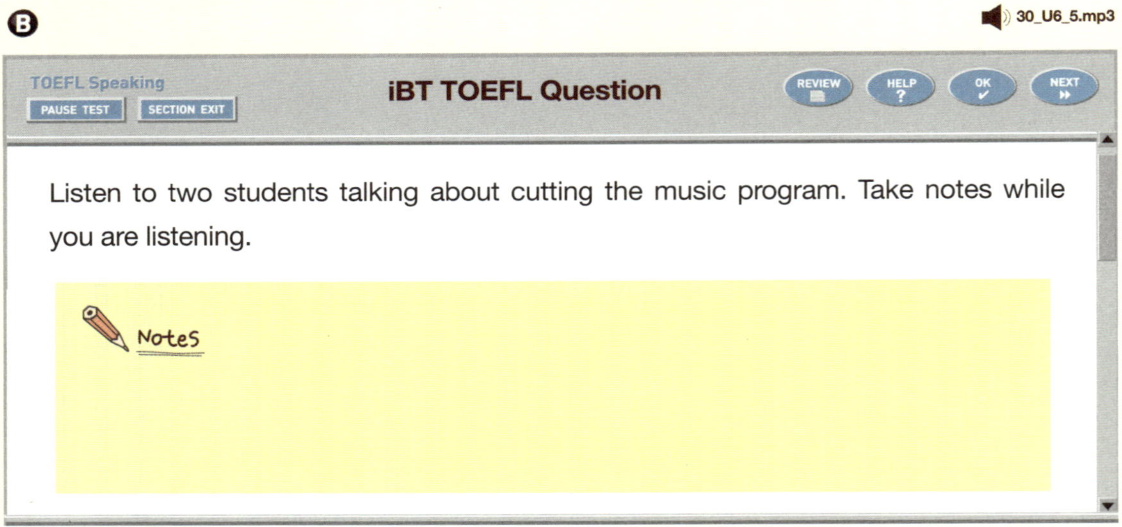

C

Referring to Ⓐ and Ⓑ, complete the outline below for a clear response.

Ⓓ Referring to your outline, create your own response to the question using the key expressions below. Make sure you time while you speak.

How long did it take for you to answer the question?

Response time:

Independent Task
Agree / Disagree

•• Target iBT TOEFL Question

Independent Task

Speaking

Television only has negative effects on children.
Do you agree or disagree with this opinion, and why?
Include details and examples to support your
explanation.

Integrated Task
General / Specific

•• Target iBT TOEFL Question

Integrated Task

Reading-Listening-Speaking

The professor talks about personal space.
With reference to the points in the lecture, explain what
is meant by this term.

:: Independent Task - Agree / Disagree

○ **I agree / disagree with the opinion that ...**

> **e.g.** I **agree with the opinion that** children should watch TV with their parents.

> **e.g.** I **disagree with the opinion that** students should turn off the TV before 9 pm.

○ **may**

> **e.g.** Students **may** be influenced by celebrities.

> **e.g.** Television **may** affect people's lifestyles, too.

○ **For these reasons,**

> **e.g.** **For these reasons,** I believe that children should watch TV with their parents.

> **e.g.** **For these reasons,** I believe that students shouldn't have to turn off the TV before 9 pm.

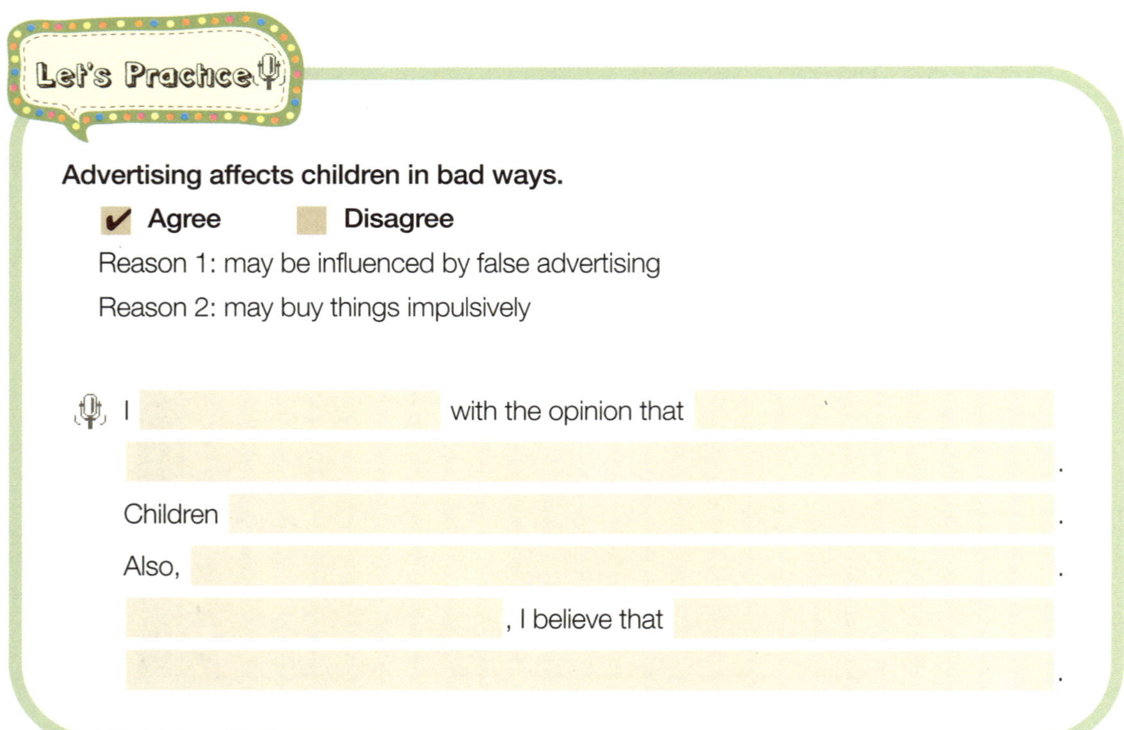

Get Started

Match the words on the left with the same meanings or synonyms on the right.

① influence •

② behavior •

③ knowledge •

④ capability •

⑤ inappropriate •

⑥ imaginative •

• ⓐ the ability to perform

• ⓑ information; a person's understanding

• ⓒ not suitable

• ⓓ effect; to affect

• ⓔ creative

• ⓕ act; conduct

Get Ready

🅐 **Answer the following questions.**

1 Do you like watching TV?

☐ Yes   ☐ No

2 How often do you watch TV a day?

☐ less than 1 hour   ☐ 1-3 hours   ☐ more than 3 hours

3 Do you think TV affects you in bad ways?

☐ Yes   ☐ A little   ☐ No

 Choose whether you agree or disagree with the following opinion. Then check (✔) two reasons. You may add your own answer.

Television only has negative effects on children.

Agree	☐ Children may be influenced by violence and degrading images on TV. ☐ TV takes time away from other activities. ☐ TV is bad for children's eyes. ☐ TV makes children want to copy actor's behavior shown on TV. ☐ TV is too unrealistic. ☐
Disagree	☐ TV helps broaden a child's knowledge base. ☐ TV provides good educational programs and news. ☐ Children learn more when they do something fun. ☐ Children do not always copy actor's behavior shown on TV. ☐

Practice Speaking

I ________________ with the opinion that television only has negative effects on children. There are two reasons why I ________________ with that opinion. First, ________________

Second, ________________

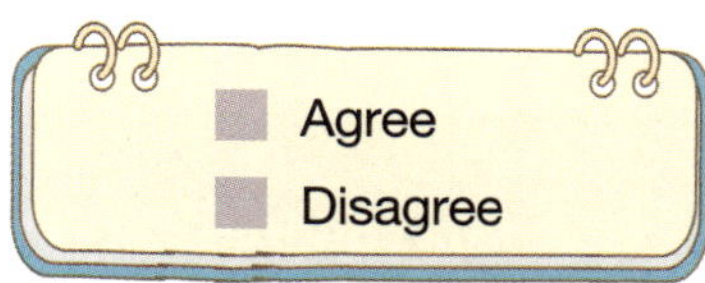

C Check (✔) your opinion on television and write the two reasons you have chosen in **B**. Then using the idea tip below as a guide, add specific details to support your two reasons.

Idea Tip

- without reading & exercising → not be able to gather knowledge and stay healthy
- have (no) capability to tell what is right and wrong
- many inappropriate scenes for children
- may learn something on TV that children may never learn in the classroom
- provide a fun and active way of learning
- become more creative and imaginative
- pay more attention

Speak Up

Referring from Ⓐ to Ⓒ, make your response to the question below.

Television only has negative effects on children. Do you agree or disagree with this opinion, and why? Include details and examples to support your explanation.

I ____________ with the opinion that television only has negative effects on children. There are two reasons why I ____________ with that opinion.

First, ____________

Second, ____________

For these reasons, I believe that ____________

Listen to the sample responses and complete the notes below.

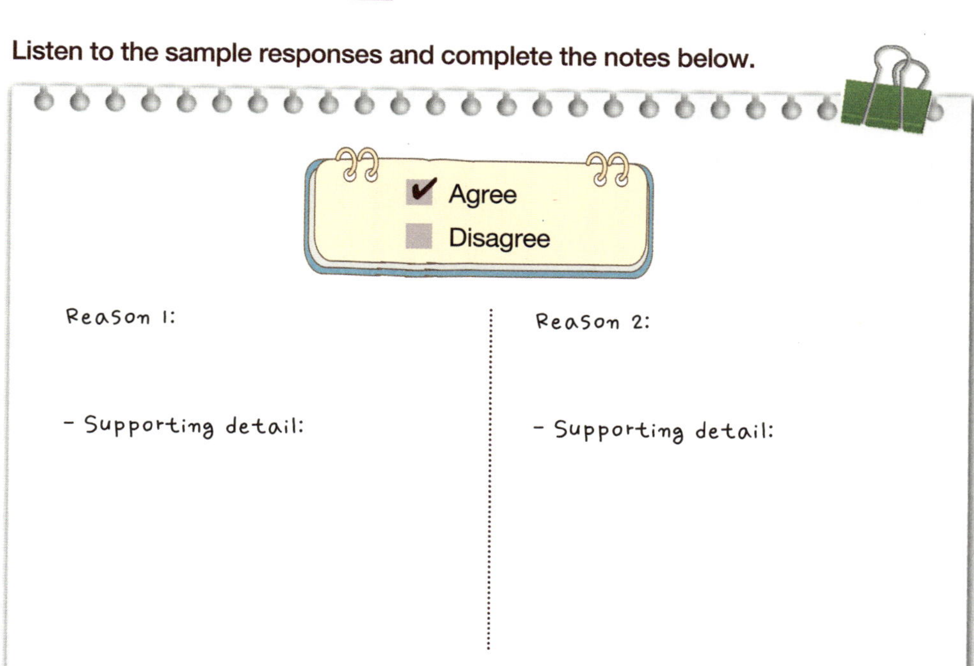

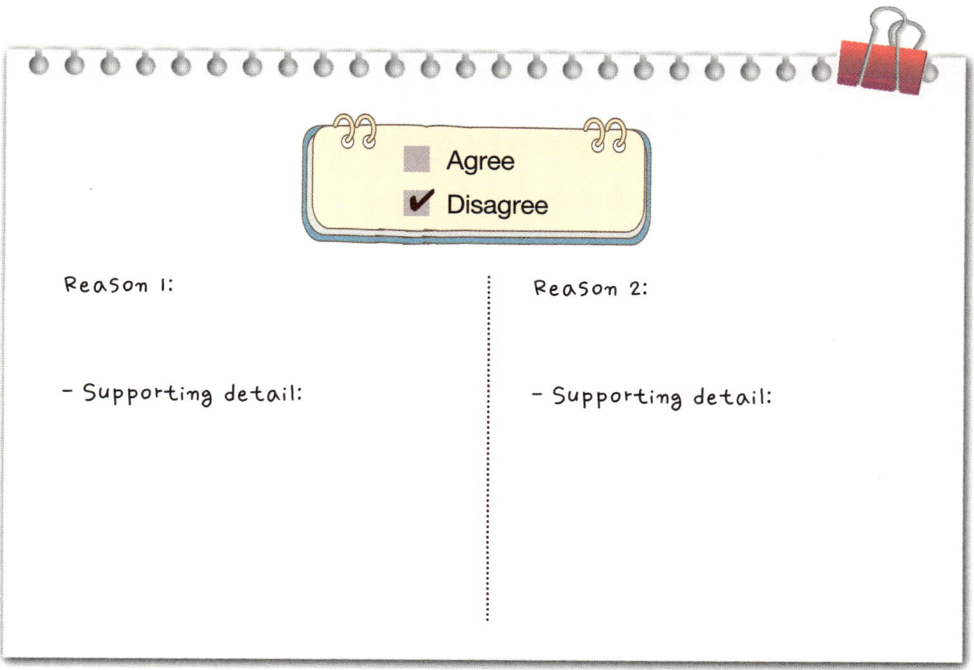

UNIT 7

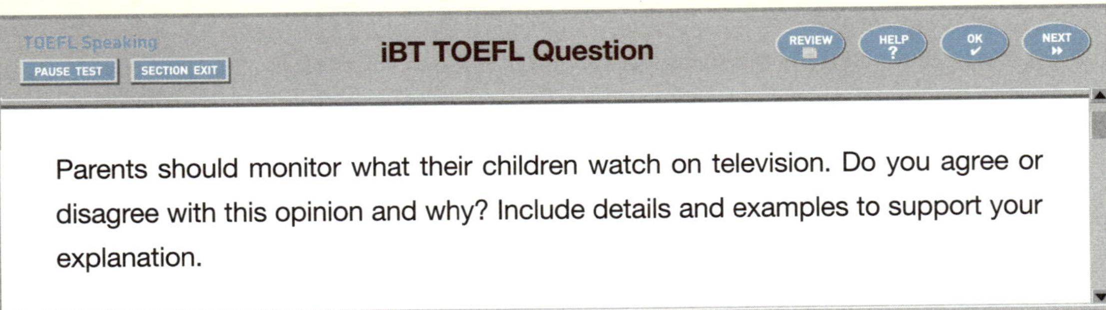

A Using the ideas below as a guide to find two major reasons, complete the outline on the next page for a response.

Agree

- For children, it is hard to make right decisions.
- Children have young minds.
- Children are still young to fight against temptation.
- Children must learn what is right and wrong.

Disagree

- Children can control over their needs.
- Parents should encourage children to become self-reliant and independent decision makers.
- Children want to do whatever they want anyway.
- Parent supervision makes children more rebellious.

Agree

Disagree

Reason 1:

- Supporting detail:

Reason 2:

- Supporting detail:

ⓑ Referring to your outline, create your own response to the question using the key expressions below. Make sure you time while you speak.

- I agree / disagree with the opinion that ...
- There are two reasons why ...
- First, ...
- Second, ...
- For these reasons, I believe that ...

How long did it take for you to answer the question?

Response time:

Integrated Task - General / Specific

General

- **The professor first points out that ...**
  - **e.g.** The professor first points out that child obesity is one of the most serious social issues.

- **The second point the professor makes is that ...**
  - **e.g.** The second point the professor makes is that bullying is another one of the most serious social issues.

Specific

- **The professor gives an example of ...**
  - **e.g.** The professor gives an example of Chris who only likes to eat junk food and spend time watching TV all weekend.

- **As an example, the professor talks about ...**
  - **e.g.** As an example, the professor talks about his son's friend, Eric, who was being bullied by his classmates.

Let's Practice

- **self-respect:** how much you 'like' yourself
  - **e.g.** Jesse - loves to ice skate even though she's not that good at it

- **self-esteem:** how 'highly' you think about yourself
  - **e.g.** Jay - failed in the final round of the dance competition

    decides to work harder to achieve his goal in the next competition

                              that self-respect is

                        . The professor gives

of Jesse who   .

The second

that self-esteem is   .

As an example,

who

but   .

Get Started

Choose the word from the box that best completes the sentence.

- uncomfortable
- access
- invisible
- tension
- close
- density
- allow
- arm-in-arm

1 Catherine is my best friend. She is really ________________ to me.

2 My best friend and I like to walk ________________ on the street.

3 On a cloudy day, the sun is ________________ to our eyes.

4 Paul and Sam never talk to each other. There's always ________________ between them.

5 I feel very ________________ when a stranger acts friendly to me.

6 It is known that Seoul has a high population ________________ .

7 I ________________ ed my friends to sleep over at my house yesterday.

8 Only those who have a keycard can have ________________ to this building.

Get Ready

A-1 Read the passage about personal space. Underline what personal space is.

Personal Space

Personal space is an invisible boundary around a person. It is thought of as a person's own territory. If someone else enters this personal territory, it may cause discomfort. On the other hand, people sometimes feel uneasy if the boundary of this territory is too large. Sometimes, people feel they need a lot of personal space; at other times, they feel comfortable with less space. These differences depend on many factors, such as intimacy and cultural standards.

A-2 Referring to **A-1**, complete the notes below.

- Personal Space: ①
  - = ②
    - someone else enters your personal territory → ③
    - boundary of this territory is too large → ④

  differences depend on
  - 1. ⑤
  - 2. ⑥

))) 32_U7_2.mp3

Professor: So, I guess we have all been in that awkward situation where someone is standing too close to us. We feel ① ___________ because somebody has ② ___________ our personal boundary. This boundary is often referred to as our ③ ___________. Personal space gets wider or narrower depending on two factors. The first is ④ ___________. The degree of intimacy we feel towards people determines how ⑤ ___________ we allow them to get to us. For example, when two people are in a romantic relationship, they each ⑥ ___________ the other ⑦ ___________ to this personal space. However, when two people have just met, and one person comes very close to the other person's face, it creates a strange ⑧ ___________. Another factor is ⑨ ___________. People from densely populated areas, such as ⑩ ___________ or ⑪ ___________, require ⑫ ___________ personal space than people from countries with a ⑬ ___________ population ⑭ ___________, such as ⑮ ___________ or ⑯ ___________. Have you noticed that American people often walk with ⑰ ___________ to ⑱ ___________ inches separating them from each other, even though they are best friends? On the other hand, Korean girls like to walk ⑲ ___________ if they are close friends.

🔊 33_U7_3.mp3

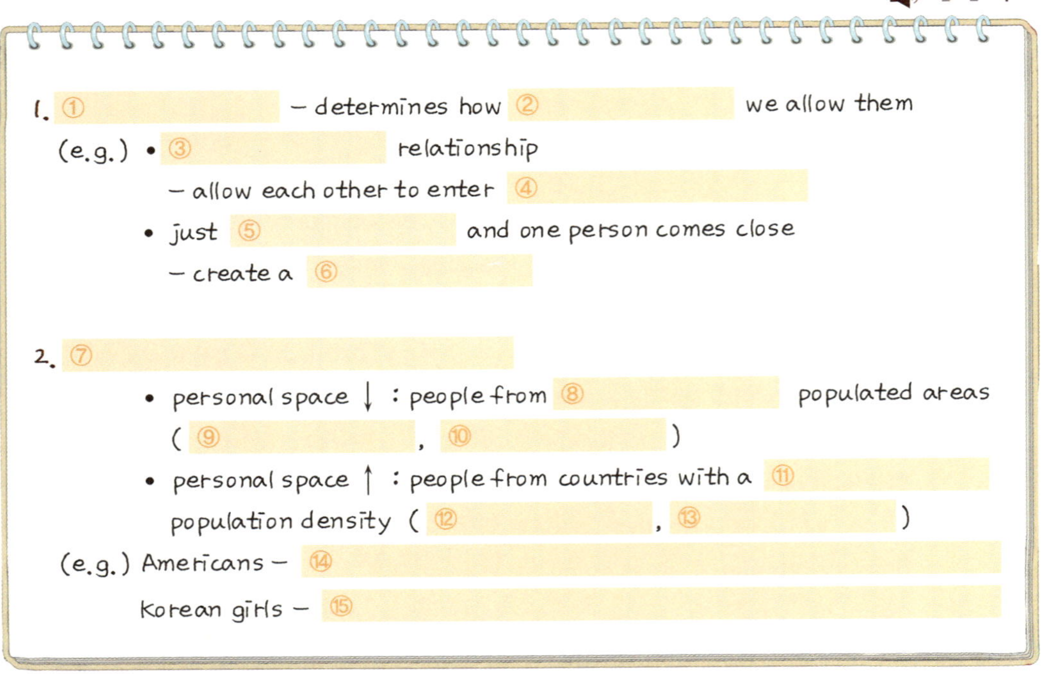

C Answer the following questions.

1 What is the lecture mainly about?

Ⓐ personal relationships Ⓑ personal space

2 What is personal space known as?

Ⓐ one's own personal territory Ⓑ one's own personal house

3 What are two factors that determine the size of one's of personal space?

__________ and __________

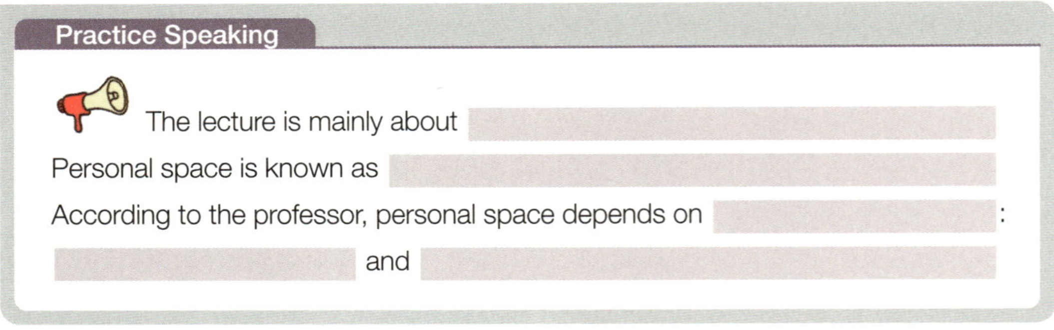

Practice Speaking

The lecture is mainly about __________

Personal space is known as __________

According to the professor, personal space depends on __________ :

__________ and __________

		True	False
1	Intimacy is the closeness one person feels to another person.	☐	☐
2	The professor gives an example of friends walking arm-in-arm as an example of intimacy.	☐	☐
3	When people do not share intimacy, they allow each other to enter their personal space.	☐	☐
4	Cultural standards also influence how much personal space a person needs.	☐	☐
5	As an example of cultural standards, the professor talks about population density.	☐	☐
6	In low-density places like America, people usually keep a distance when walking with friends.	☐	☐
7	In high-density places like Korea, girls often link arms with their friends.	☐	☐

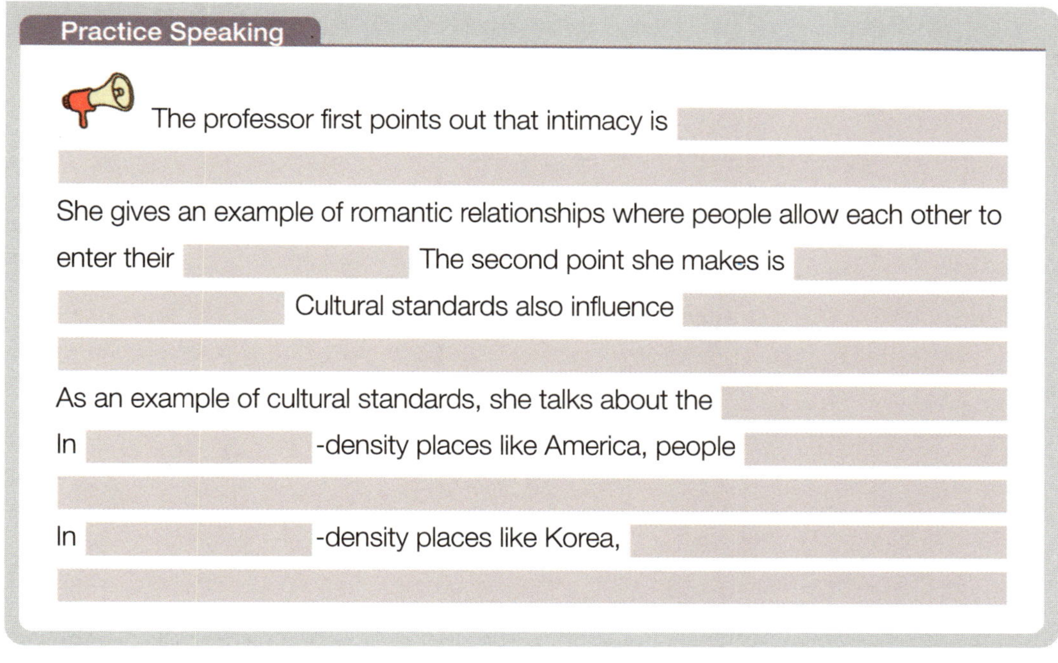

Practice Speaking

The professor first points out that intimacy is ______________

____

She gives an example of romantic relationships where people allow each other to enter their ______________ The second point she makes is ______________

______________ Cultural standards also influence ______________

____

As an example of cultural standards, she talks about the ______________

In ______________-density places like America, people ______________

____

In ______________-density places like Korea, ______________

____

Speak Up 

Referring from Ⓐ to Ⓓ, make your response to the question below.

> **The professor talks about personal space. With reference to the points in the lecture, explain what is meant by this term.**

The lecture is mainly about   Personal space is

known as   According to the professor, personal

space depends on   :

and   The professor first points out that

intimacy is

She gives an example of

The second point she makes is   Cultural

standards also influence

As an example of cultural standards, she talks about

In   -density places like America,

In   -density places like Korea,

 **Check Your Response**  34_U7_4.mp3

Listen to the sample response and take notes if necessary.

Ⓐ Read the passage about verbal and nonverbal signals.

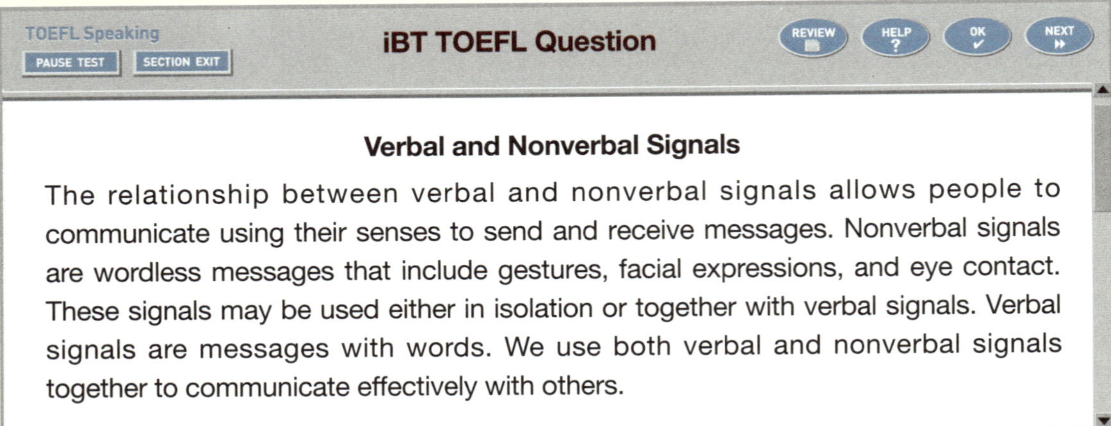

Ⓑ 🔊 35_U7_5.mp3

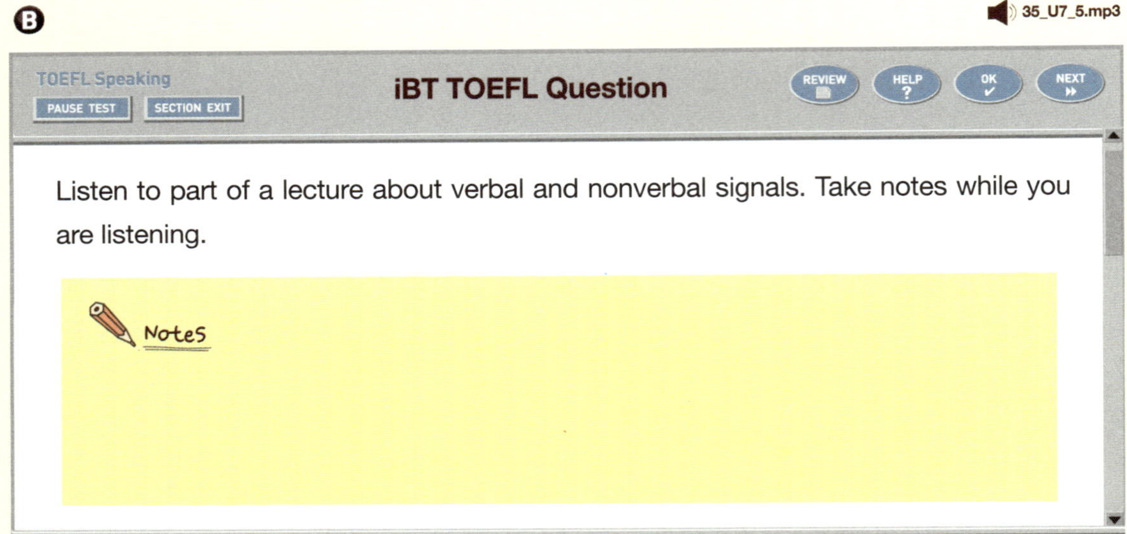

Ⓒ

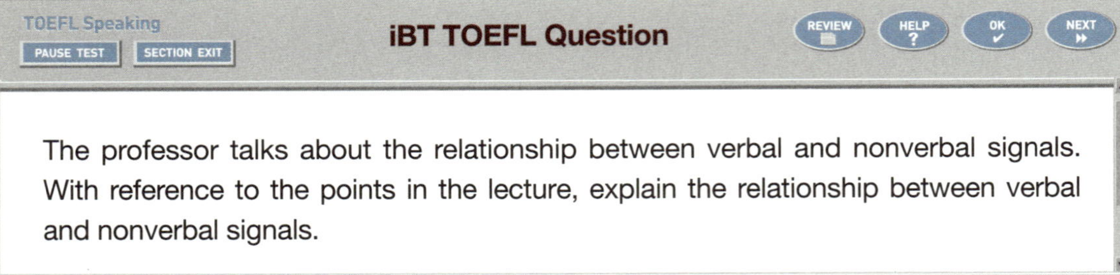

Referring to **Ⓐ** and **Ⓑ**, complete the outline below.

Main point: relationship between verbal and nonverbal signals

- Verbal signals:

- Nonverbal signals:

1. verbal & nonverbal signals show the same meanings
   - (e.g.)

2. verbal & nonverbal signals show conflicting meanings
   - (e.g.)

Ⓓ Referring to your outline, create your own response to the question using the key expressions below. Make sure you time while you speak.

- The lecture is mainly about ...
- According to the professor, ...
- The professor first points out that ...
- He gives an example of a time when he ...
- The second point he makes is that ...
- As an example of ..., he talks about ...

How long did it take for you to answer the question?

Response time:

Independent Task
Agree / Disagree

•• Target iBT TOEFL Question

Independent Task

Speaking

People behave differently depending on what type of clothing they wear.
Do you agree or disagree with this statement, and why?
Include details and examples to support your explanation.

Integrated Task
General / Specific

•• Target iBT TOEFL Question

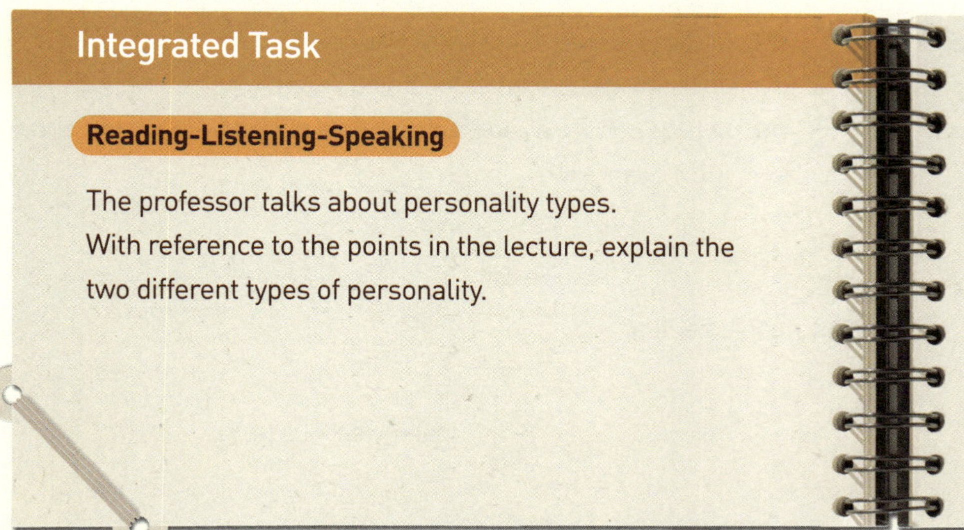

Integrated Task

Reading-Listening-Speaking

The professor talks about personality types.
With reference to the points in the lecture, explain the
two different types of personality.

Independent Task - Agree / Disagree

- **I believe that ...**

  e.g. I believe that teachers motivate students to do well.

- **One of the reasons is that ...**

  e.g. One of the reasons is that teachers have the ability to raise students' grade.

- **The other reason is that ...**

  e.g. The other reason is that students can concentrate well when a teacher is good-looking or pretty.

- **For example, ... / For instance, ...**

  e.g. For example, I study English very hard to impress my teacher.

  e.g. For instance, my History teacher tells us history tales every day.

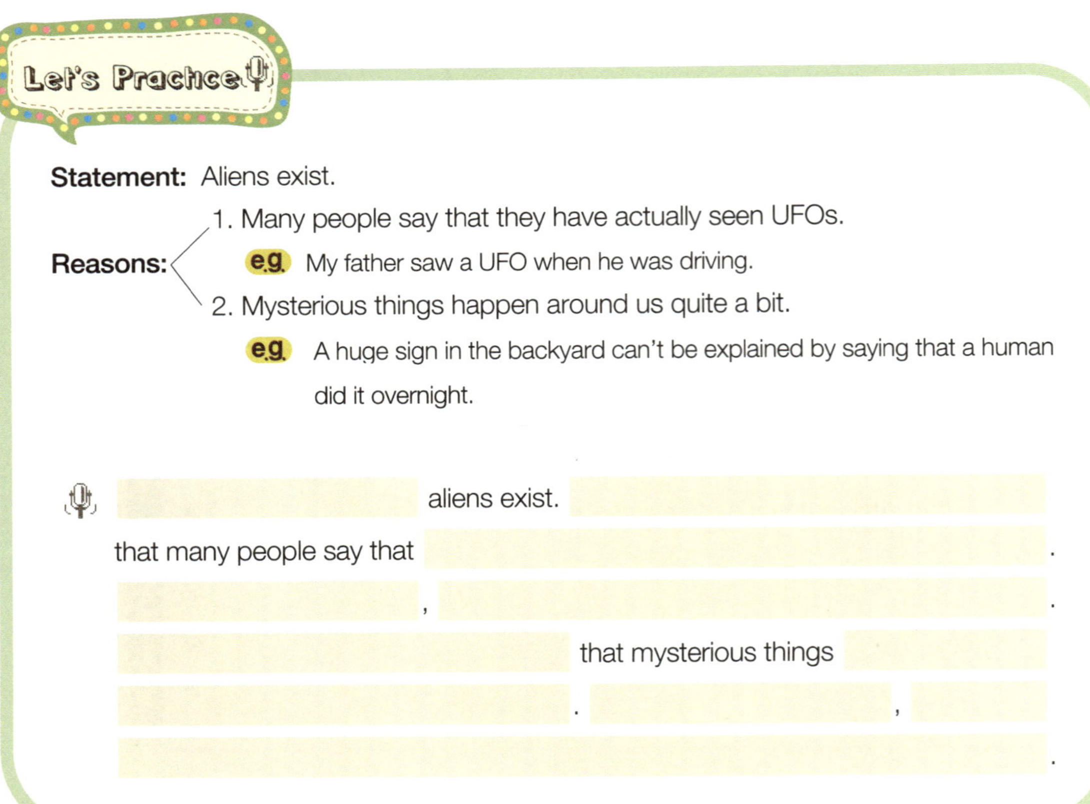

Let's Practice

Statement: Aliens exist.

Reasons:
1. Many people say that they have actually seen UFOs.

   e.g. My father saw a UFO when he was driving.

2. Mysterious things happen around us quite a bit.

   e.g. A huge sign in the backyard can't be explained by saying that a human did it overnight.

_______________ aliens exist. _______________

that many people say that _______________ .

_______________ , _______________ .

_______________ that mysterious things

_______________ . _______________ ,

_______________ .

Get Started

Match the words with the appropriate definitions.

① habit   •

② respect   •

③ confident   •

④ fixed   •

⑤ different   •

⑥ behave   •

• ⓐ having strong belief or full assurance

• ⓑ attached or already set upon something

• ⓒ a behavior pattern that is hard to change

• ⓓ to act or perform

• ⓔ to show regard or honor

• ⓕ not identical; not the same

Get Ready

Ⓐ Answer the following questions.

1 What types of clothes do you like?

▢ casual clothes   ▢ formal clothes

▢ hip-hop clothes   ▢ others __________________

2 Do you think looks are important?

▢ Yes   ▢ No

3 Does your behavior change depending on what type of clothes you wear?

▢ Yes   ▢ No

4 Do you usually judge people by what types of clothes they wear?

▢ Yes   ▢ No

Ⓑ Choose one of the following statements you agree with. Then check (✓) two reasons. You may add your own answer.

> ☐ **People behave differently depending on what type of clothing they wear.**
>
> ☐ A person's feelings may change depending on colors or styles of the clothes.
>
> ☐ Looks have an effect on how people act.
>
> ☐ People tend to treat a person differently depending on the type of clothing they wear.
>
> ☐

> ☐ **People do not behave differently depending on what type of clothing they wear.**
>
> ☐ Clothes themselves do not affect the way people act.
>
> ☐ Most people do not care about what others think.
>
> ☐ A person's habits or character does not change that easily.
>
> ☐

Practice Speaking

I believe that people ____________________ depending on what type of clothing they wear. There are two reasons why I believe this. One of the reasons is that ____________________ The other reason is that ____________________

Ⓒ Check (✓) your opinion on people behavior depending on what types of clothing they wear and write two reasons you have chosen in Ⓑ. Then using the idea tip below as a guide, add specific details to support your two reasons.

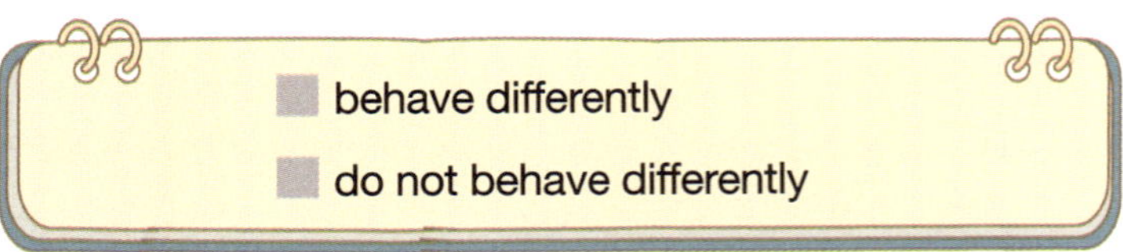

Reason 1	Reason 2
– Supporting detail	– Supporting detail

- wear baggy clothes → speak like rappers and walk differently
- treat a person with respect / think highly of oneself / feel confident
- consider time, places and occasion (e.g. funeral, club, school, etc)
- behave differently when I am wearing a suit or casual clothes
- act differently because people feel different, not because of their clothes
- my behavior does not change because of what I am wearing
- can still behave like a rapper with a gentle suit on
- a fixed habit → clothing never has to do with behavior

UNIT 8

Practice Speaking

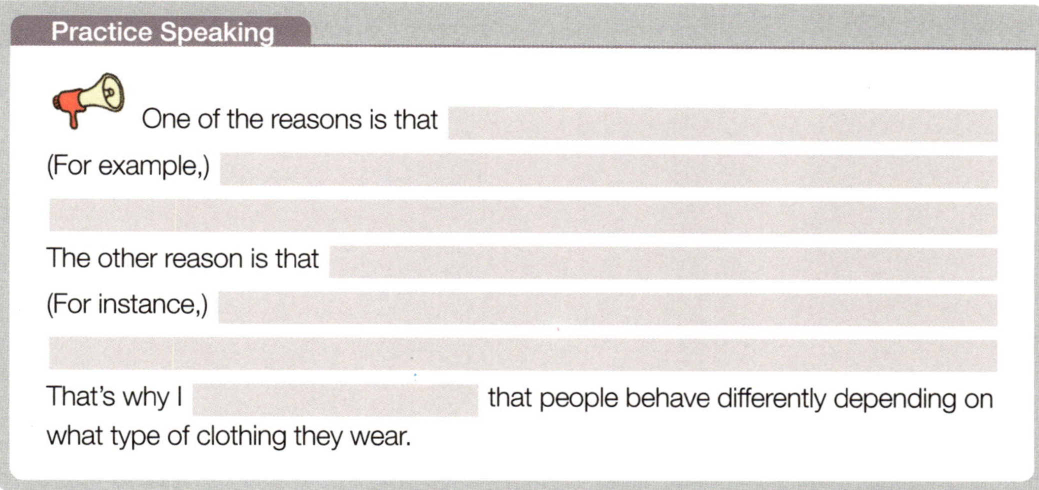

One of the reasons is that ________

(For example,) ________

____

The other reason is that ________

(For instance,) ________

____

That's why I ________ that people behave differently depending on what type of clothing they wear.

Speak Up

People behave differently depending on what type of clothing they wear. Do you agree or disagree with this statement, and why? Include details and examples to support your explanation.

I believe that people

There are two reasons why I believe this. One of the reasons is that

(For example,)

The other reason is that

(For instance,)

That's why I   that people behave differently depending on what type of clothing they wear.

Check Your Response 🔊 36_U8_1.mp3

Listen to the sample responses and complete the notes below.

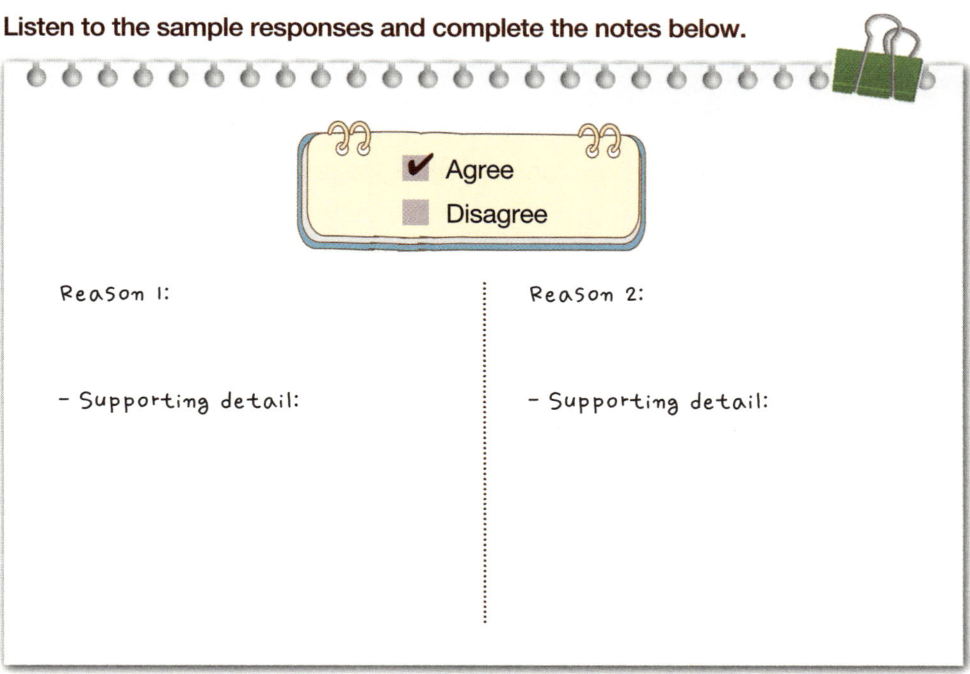

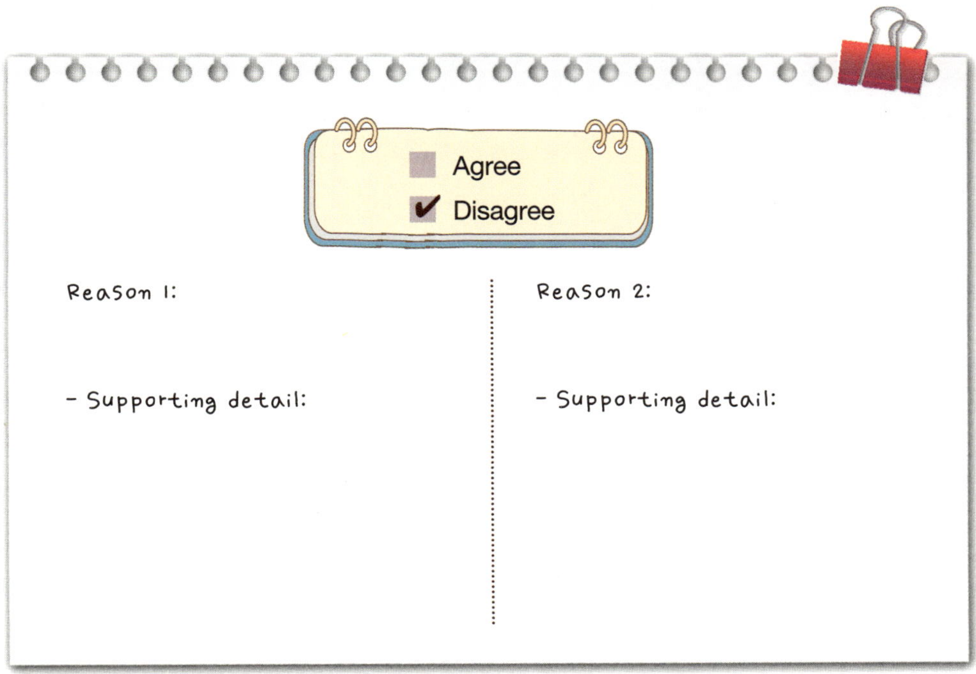

UNIT 8

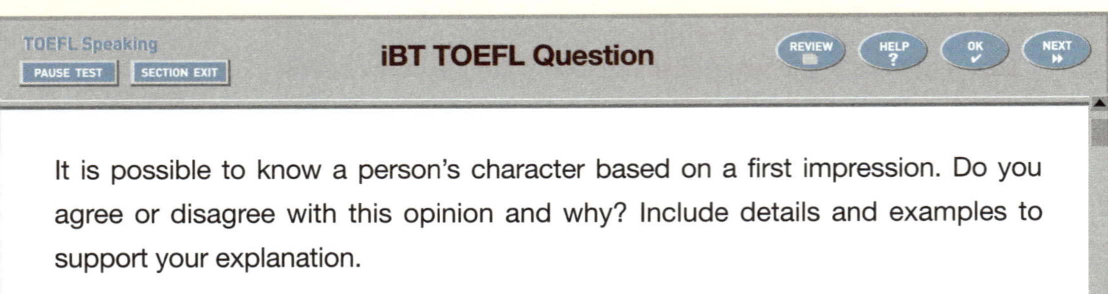

A Using the ideas below as a guide to find two major reasons, complete the outline on the next page for a response.

☐ possible to know

- I can usually tell people's personalities by their appearance.
- It's hard to completely change who you are, even if only for a brief introduction.
- People are more likely to be themselves upon first meeting.
- First impressions cannot be completely ignored.

☐ impossible to know

- A first impression depends mainly on external looks.
- It is too hasty to judge people on their first impression.
- Some people act differently when they first meet new people.
- People can be influenced by their mood or feelings that day.

possible to know

impossible to know

Reason 1:

- Supporting detail:

Reason 2:

- Supporting detail:

B Referring to your outline, create your own response to the question using the key expressions below. Make sure you time while you speak.

- I believe that it is possible / impossible to know ...
- There are two reasons why I believe this.
- One of the reasons is that ...
- For example, ...
- The other reason is that ...
- For instance, ...
- That's why I agree / disagree that ...

How long did it take for you to answer the question?

 Response time:

UNIT 8

Integrated Task - General / Specific

give up V-ing / N (V = Verb, N = Noun)

> *e.g.* I promise to **give up being** late every morning.

> *e.g.* Do not **give up hope**.

enjoy V-ing (V = Verb)

> *e.g.* I **enjoy hanging** out with my friends.

by V-ing (V = Verb)

> *e.g.* We got to know each other well **by playing** games together.

have time to oneself

> *e.g.* Try to **have time to yourself**, even though you have so much work to do.

believe in oneself

> *e.g.* People with high self-esteem **believe in themselves**.

get rid of

> *e.g.* I hope I can **get rid of** my fixed habit of biting my nails.

Let's Practice

1. I've changed my personality by ____________ social gatherings. (attend)

2. We enjoy ____________ our old school days when we meet. (talk about)

3. I gave up ____________ cruel to my younger brother. (be)

4. If you want somebody else to believe you, then you need to ____________ first.

5. When you feel so exhausted, you definitely need to ____________ .

Get Started

Match each word with the correct definition.

① reserved   <u>j</u>   ⓐ **adj** enjoy new things with risks

② shy   ⓑ **v** to manage; to deal with

③ energetic   ⓒ **adj** feel safe around

④ adventurous   ⓓ **adj** powerful in action

⑤ asocial   ⓔ **adj** to feel relaxed and less worried

⑥ restore   ⓕ **v** to let go

⑦ release   ⓖ **v** to give back

⑧ handle   ⓗ **v** to go out and spend time outside

⑨ reflect   ⓘ **adj** timid and lack of confidence

⑩ secure   ⓙ **adj** avoid closeness with others and being careful

⑪ hang out   ⓚ **v** to think deeply about something

⑫ comfort   ⓛ **adj** not sociable

Get Ready

A-1 Read the passage about personality types. Underline two different types of personality.

Personality Types

Generally speaking, people can be divided into two common personality types: introverts and extroverts. Introverted personality types are considered to be reserved, shy, and less outgoing. Extroverted types, in comparison, are seen as very social, energetic, and adventurous. Introverts are not completely asocial, but they are far less likely to make new social contacts. In times of stress, introverts tend to restore their energy through deep thought. Extroverts, on the other hand, find comfort in being around other people and tend to release energy.

A-2 Referring to **A-1**, complete the notes below.

```
* Personality types :
    1. ①                    : reserved, ②                  , less ③
                             less likely to make ④
    2. ⑤                    : social, ⑥                  , ⑦

    (e.g.) in times of stress ...
        — introverts : ⑧
        — extroverts : ⑨
```

B-1 Listen to part of a lecture about personality types. Fill in the blanks to complete the lecture.

◀)) 37_U8_2.mp3

Professor: Today, we're going to talk about ①   and ②   personality types and the different ways in which these types of people handle ③   . How many of you would consider yourselves to be ④   or ⑤   ? Do you know the difference? Well, introverts are people who like to spend time ⑥   . When they get ⑦   , they like to be ⑧   and have space to ⑨   . An example of an introverted individual is my friend, Crystal. When Crystal is stressed out, she likes to stay home where she can read books, take baths, and have time to ⑩   on her own ⑪   . She feels ⑫   and ⑬   when she has time to ⑭   . If you can see a bit of yourself in Crystal, you may have an introverted personality type. On the other hand, extroverts are more ⑮   by nature and enjoy the company of ⑯   . When they get stressed out, they like to go ⑰   . My friend, Charles, is an example of an extroverted personality type. When Charles gets stressed out, he enjoys hanging out with his friends and being in ⑱   groups. After a long day at work, Charles enjoys playing ⑲   with his friends and going to ⑳   . He finds it more ㉑   and enjoyable to be around others. If you are like Charles, then you would be considered an extrovert.

B-2 Listen to the lecture again. Without looking at **B-1** , complete the notes on two types of personalities.

◀)) 38_U8_3.mp3

UNIT 8

C **Answer the following questions.**

1 What is the lecture mainly about?

    Ⓐ introverted and extroverted personality types and the different ways that people who fit into these types handle stress

    Ⓑ introverted and extroverted personality types and how people who fit these types spend time

2 Put the related words or phrases that apply to the personality type under the correct categories.

Introverted personality type	Extroverted personality type

shy   social   reserved

confident   less outgoing   adventurous

have fewer friends

restore their energy through deep thought   release energy

like to be in groups of people   like to be alone

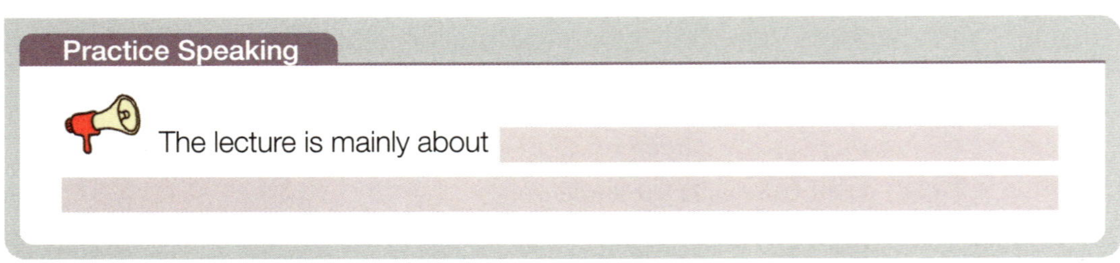

Practice Speaking

The lecture is mainly about ______________________________

 Check (✔) whether the following statements are true of false.

		True	False
1	Introverted people like to get rid of stress by going outside and hanging out with people.	☐	☐
2	The professor uses the example of her friend, Crystal, to talk about the introverted personality type.	☐	☐
3	Crystal usually relieves stress by doing things alone such as reading books and meditating.	☐	☐
4	Extroverted people like to relieve stress by spending time alone.	☐	☐
5	As an example of the extroverted personality type, the professor tells us about Crystal.	☐	☐
6	Charles relieves stress by playing basketball and hanging out with his friends at parties.	☐	☐

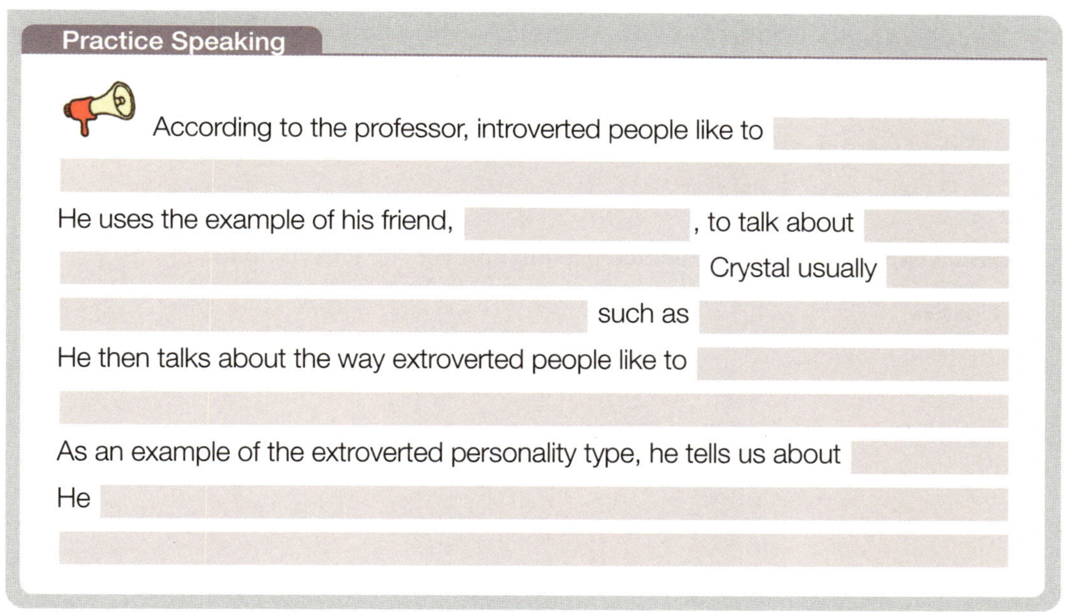

Practice Speaking

According to the professor, introverted people like to ____________
____

He uses the example of his friend, ____________, to talk about ____________
Crystal usually ____________
____________ such as ____________

He then talks about the way extroverted people like to ____________
____

As an example of the extroverted personality type, he tells us about ____________

He ____________
____

UNIT 8

Speak Up

Referring from Ⓐ to Ⓓ, make your response to the question below.

> **The professor talks about personality types. With reference to the points in the lecture, explain the two different types of personality.**

The lecture is mainly about

According to the professor, introverted people like to

He uses the example of his friend,   , to talk about

Crystal usually

He then talks about the way extroverted people like to

As an example of the extroverted personality type, he tells us about
Charles

Check Your Response

39_U8_4.mp3

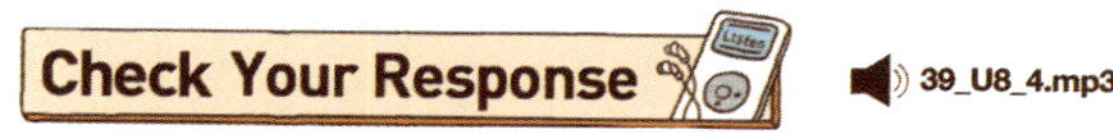

Listen to the sample response and take notes if necessary.

UNIT 8

Ⓐ Read the passage about self-esteem.

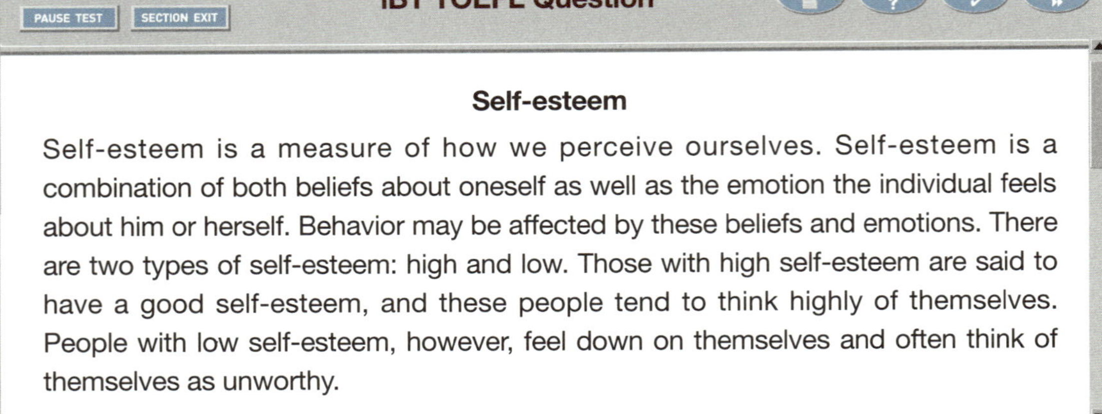

Ⓑ

🔊 40_U8_5.mp3

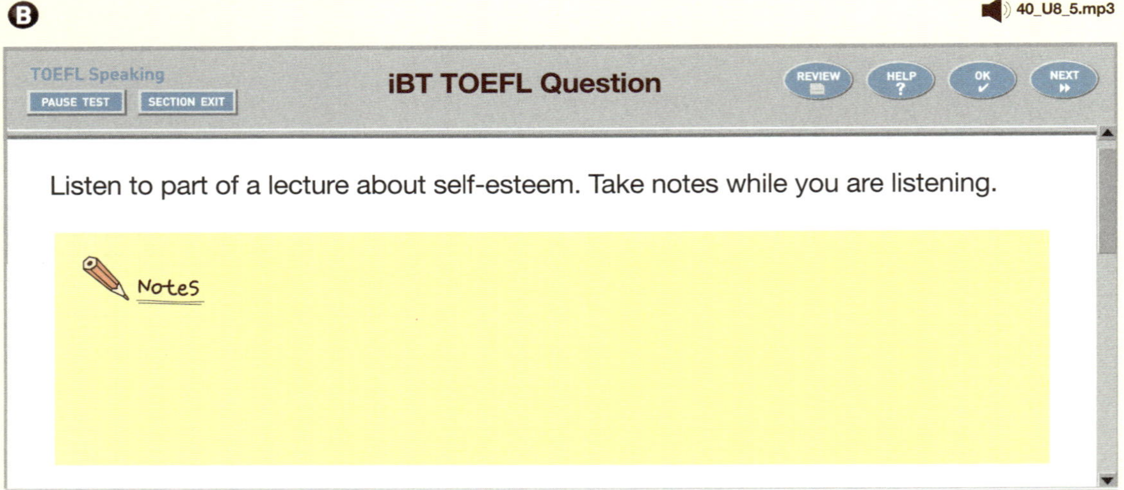

Ⓒ

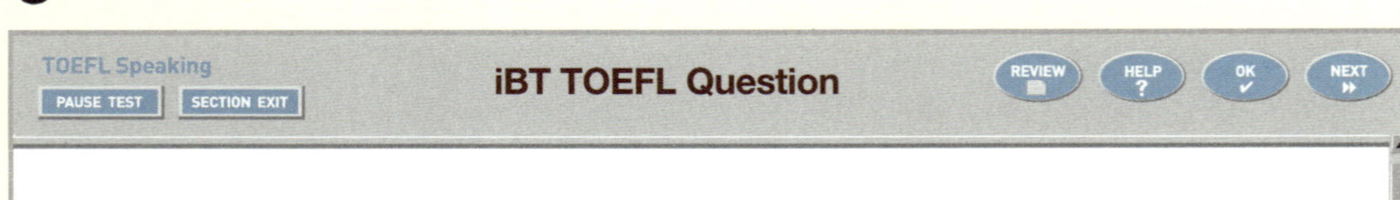

Referring to **Ⓐ** and **Ⓑ**, complete the outline below.

• **Main point:** difference between high self-esteem and low self-esteem

   – self-esteem:

   1. high self-esteem:
      – (e.g.)

   2. low self-esteem:
      – (e.g.)

Ⓓ Referring to your outline, create your own response to the question using the key expressions below. Make sure you time while you speak.

- The lecture is mainly about ...
- According to the professor, ...
- She uses the example of ... to talk about ...
- As an example of ... , she tells us about ...

How long did it take for you to answer the question?

Response time:

Actual Test

iBT TOEFL

Actual Test

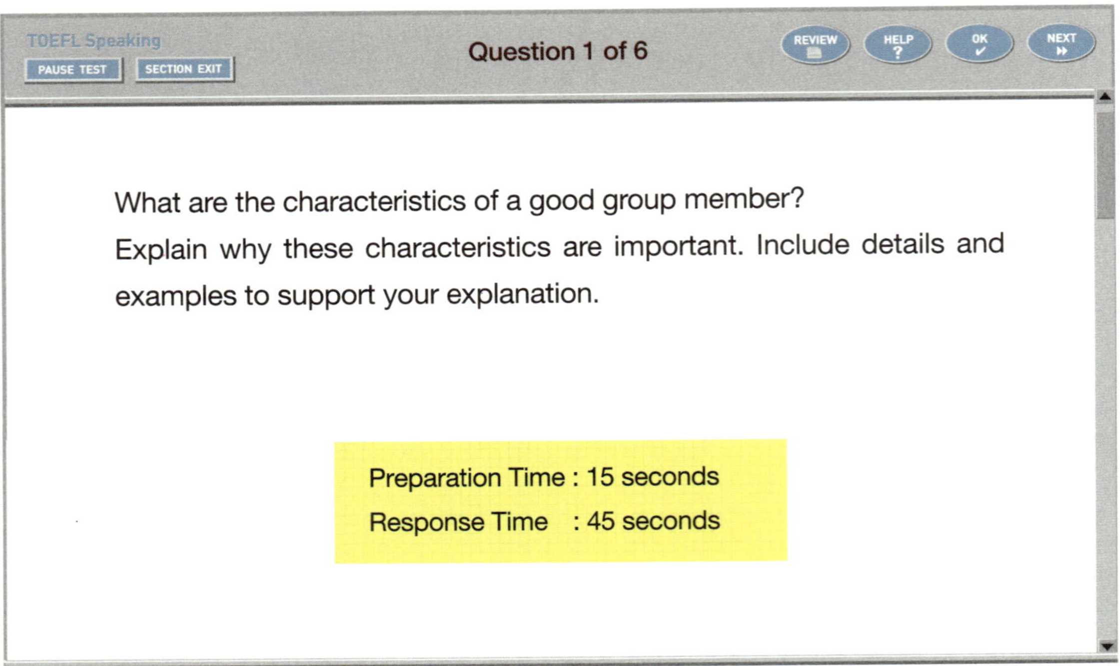

TOEFL Speaking
PAUSE TEST
SECTION EXIT
Question 1 of 6
REVIEW
HELP ?
OK ✔
NEXT ▶▶
What are the characteristics of a good group member?
Explain why these characteristics are important. Include details and examples to support your explanation.
Preparation Time : 15 seconds
Response Time   : 45 seconds

Notes

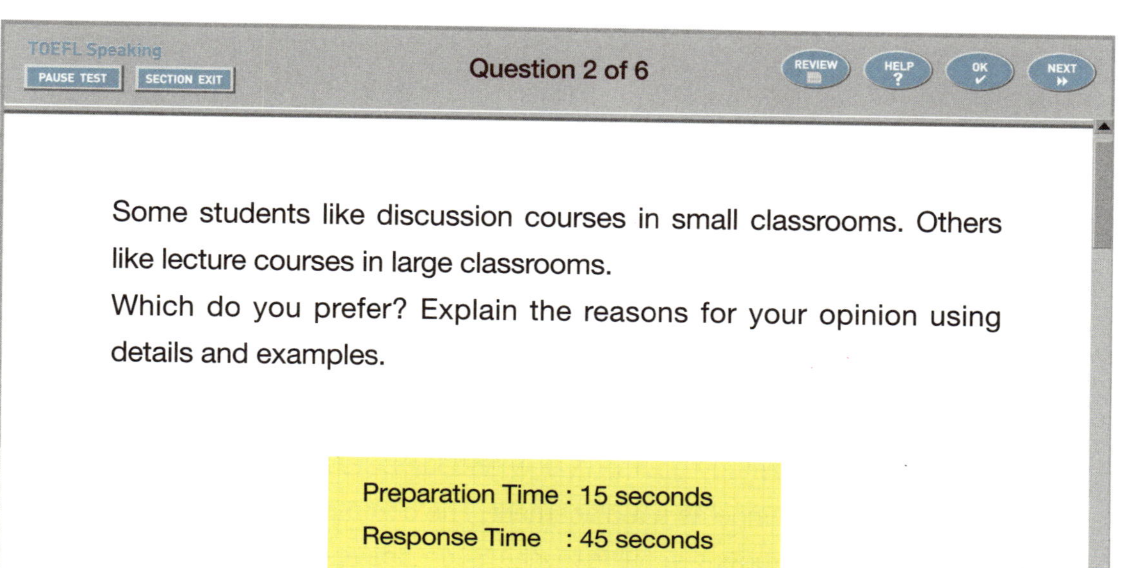

TOEFL Speaking
PAUSE TEST   SECTION EXIT
Question 2 of 6
REVIEW   HELP   OK   NEXT

Some students like discussion courses in small classrooms. Others like lecture courses in large classrooms.
Which do you prefer? Explain the reasons for your opinion using details and examples.

Preparation Time : 15 seconds
Response Time   : 45 seconds

Notes

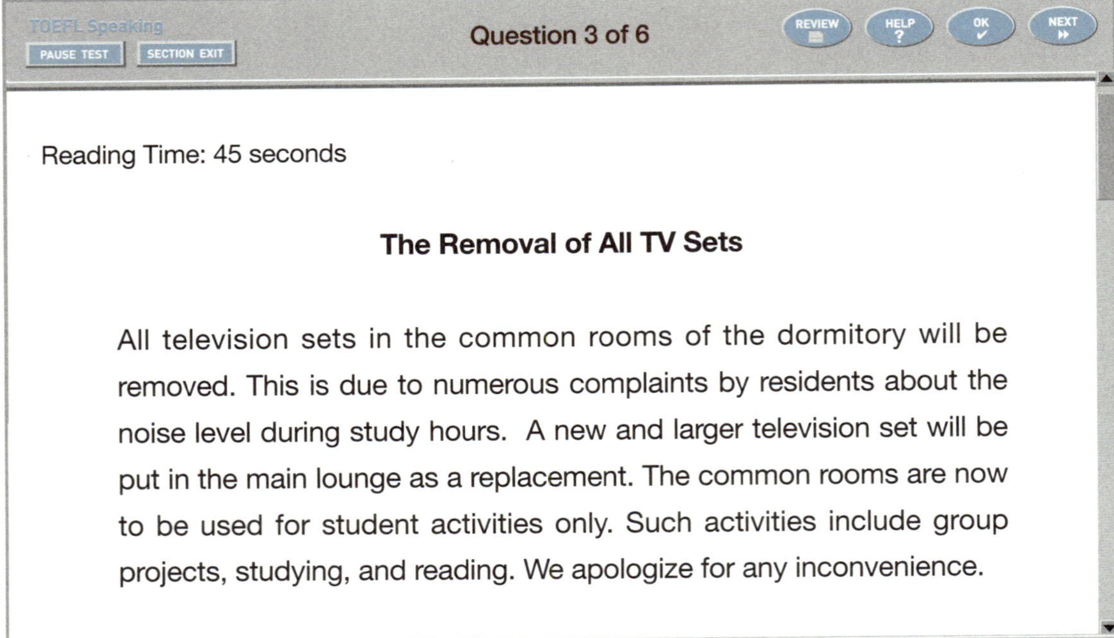
TOEFL Speaking
PAUSE TEST   SECTION EXIT
Question 3 of 6
REVIEW
HELP ?
OK ✔
NEXT ▸▸
Reading Time: 45 seconds

The Removal of All TV Sets

All television sets in the common rooms of the dormitory will be removed. This is due to numerous complaints by residents about the noise level during study hours. A new and larger television set will be put in the main lounge as a replacement. The common rooms are now to be used for student activities only. Such activities include group projects, studying, and reading. We apologize for any inconvenience.

◀)) 41_AT_3.mp3

TOEFL Speaking
PAUSE TEST   SECTION EXIT
Question 3 of 6
REVIEW
HELP ?
OK ✔
NEXT ▸▸

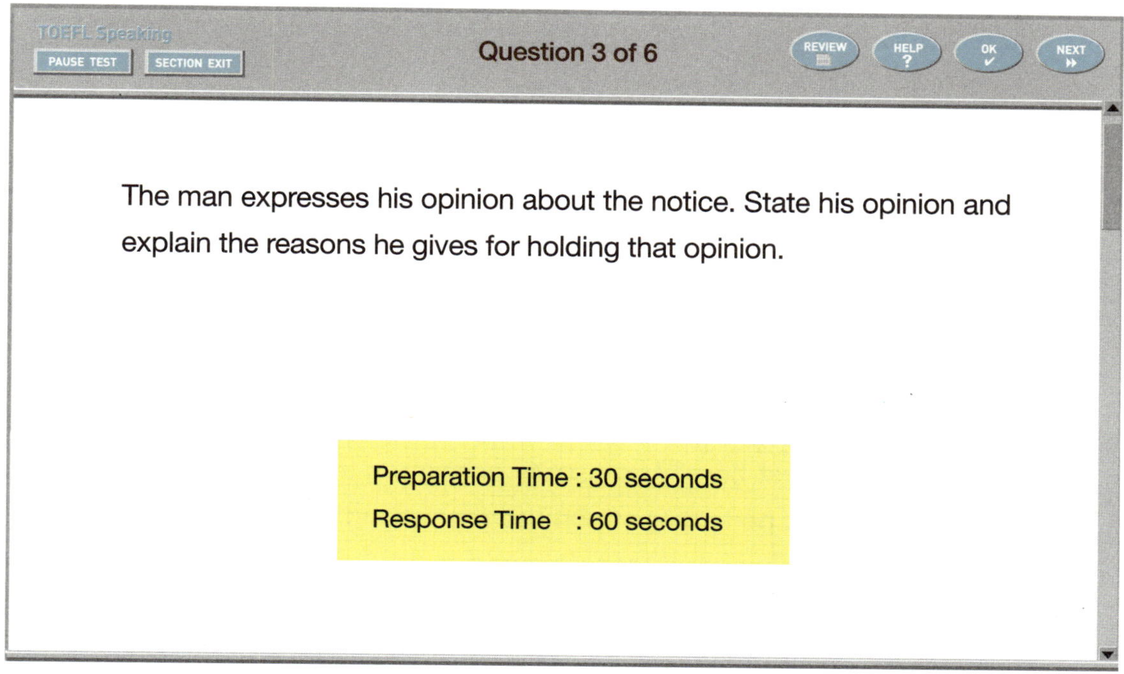
TOEFL Speaking
PAUSE TEST
SECTION EXIT
REVIEW
HELP
?
OK
✔
NEXT
▸▸
The man expresses his opinion about the notice. State his opinion and explain the reasons he gives for holding that opinion.
Preparation Time : 30 seconds
Response Time   : 60 seconds

Notes

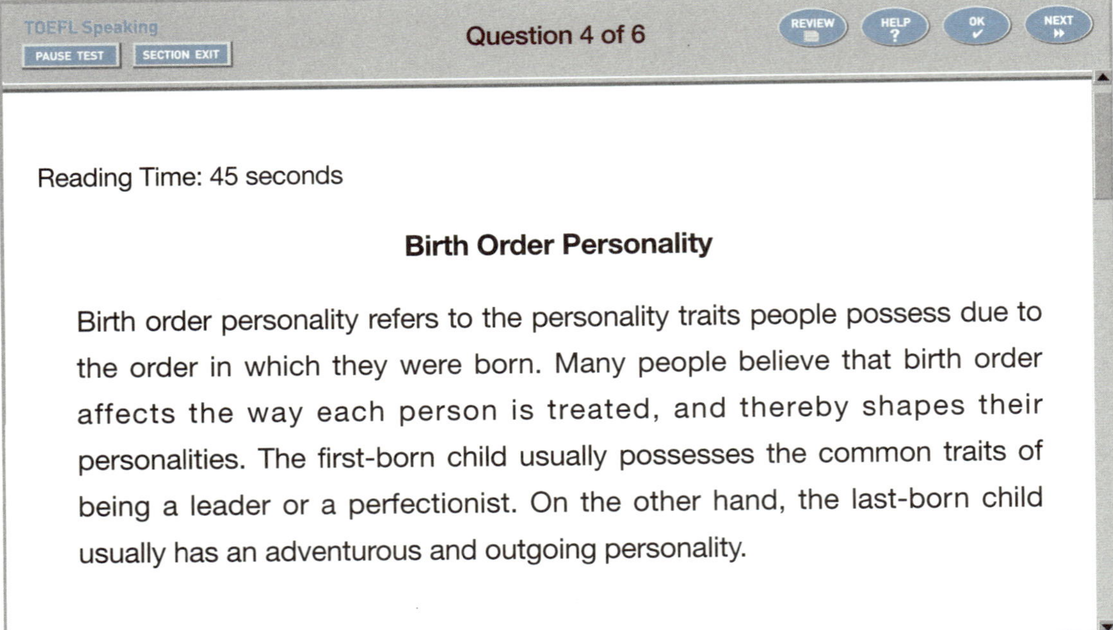

TOEFL Speaking
PAUSE TEST   SECTION EXIT
Question 4 of 6
REVIEW   HELP ?   OK ✔   NEXT ▶▶

Reading Time: 45 seconds

Birth Order Personality

Birth order personality refers to the personality traits people possess due to the order in which they were born. Many people believe that birth order affects the way each person is treated, and thereby shapes their personalities. The first-born child usually possesses the common traits of being a leader or a perfectionist. On the other hand, the last-born child usually has an adventurous and outgoing personality.

◀)) 42_AT_4.mp3

TOEFL Speaking
PAUSE TEST   SECTION EXIT
Question 4 of 6
REVIEW   HELP ?   OK ✔   NEXT ▶▶

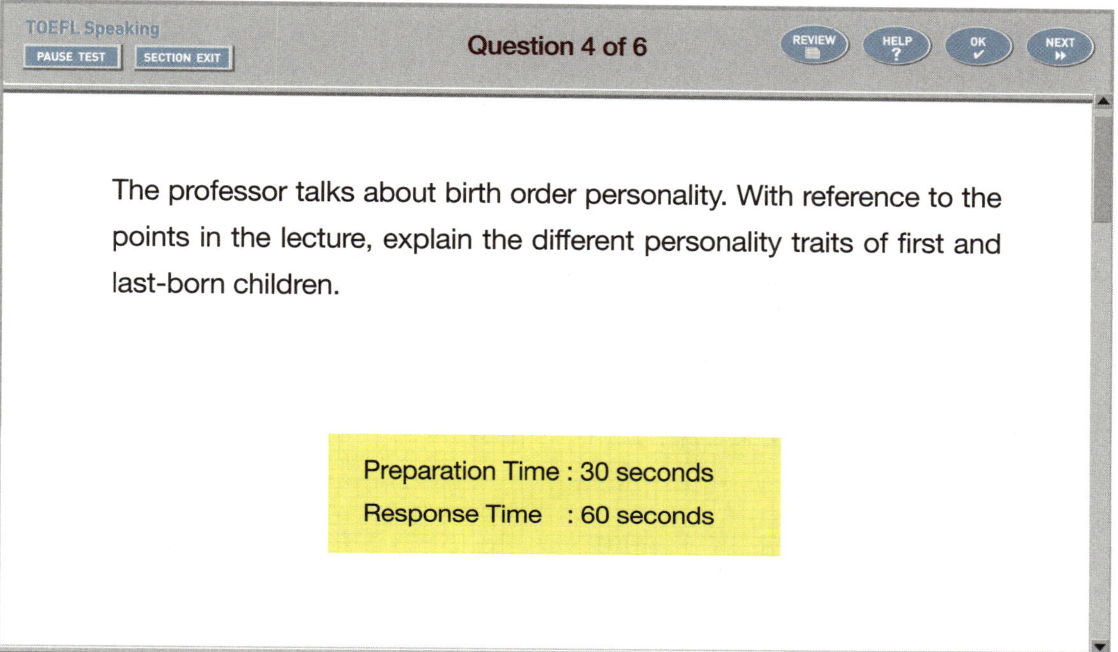
TOEFL Speaking
PAUSE TEST   SECTION EXIT
Question 4 of 6
REVIEW   HELP ?   OK ✔   NEXT ▶▶

The professor talks about birth order personality. With reference to the points in the lecture, explain the different personality traits of first and last-born children.

Preparation Time : 30 seconds
Response Time   : 60 seconds

Actual Test

Notes

TOEFL Speaking
PAUSE TEST   SECTION EXIT
Question 5 of 6
REVIEW   HELP ?   OK ✓   NEXT ▸▸

Notes

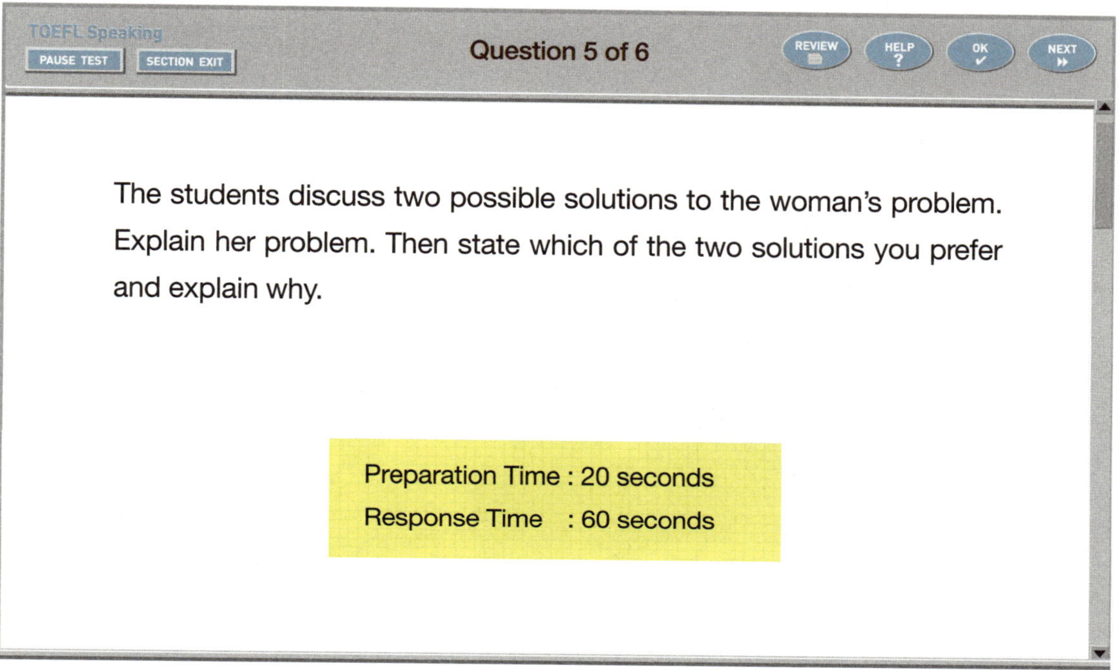
TOEFL Speaking
PAUSE TEST
SECTION EXIT
Question 5 of 6
REVIEW
HELP
?
OK
✓
NEXT
▶▶
The students discuss two possible solutions to the woman's problem. Explain her problem. Then state which of the two solutions you prefer and explain why.
Preparation Time : 20 seconds
Response Time   : 60 seconds

Notes

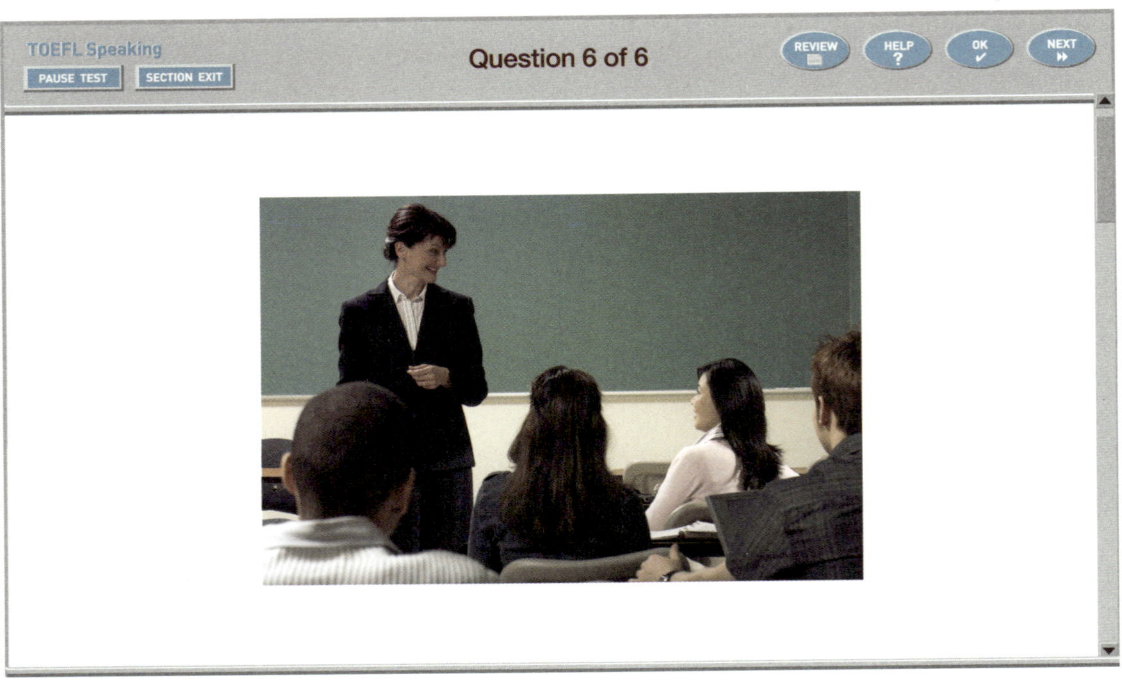

TOEFL Speaking
PAUSE TEST   SECTION EXIT
Question 6 of 6
REVIEW
HELP ?
OK ✓
NEXT ▸▸

Notes

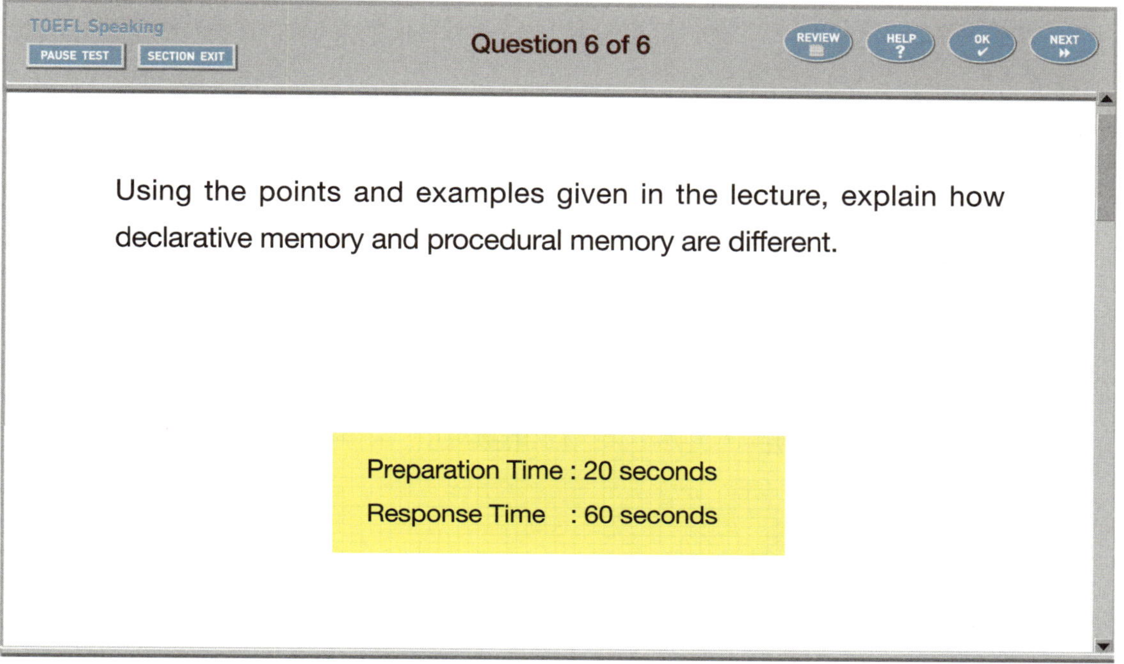

Using the points and examples given in the lecture, explain how declarative memory and procedural memory are different.

Preparation Time : 20 seconds
Response Time   : 60 seconds

Notes

Wit&Wisdom iBT TOEFL Series

Beginning (40~60) · Intermediate (60~90)

The iBT TOEFL Beginner Series

 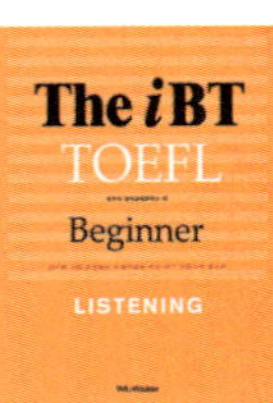  

★ **The iBT TOEFL Beginner**
Reading / Listening / Speaking / Writing

Perium VOCA Series

  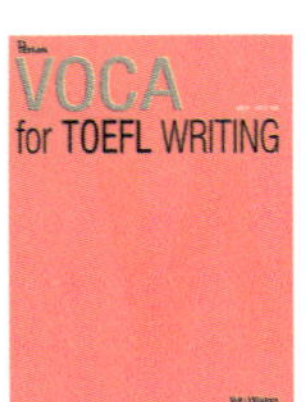

★★ **Perium VOCA for TOEFL**
Reading / Speaking / Writing

The iBT TOEFL Series

   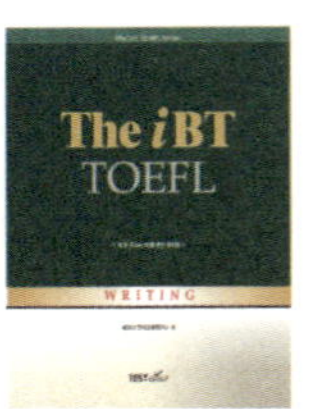

★★ **The iBT TOEFL**
Reading / Listening / Speaking / Writing

The iBT Grammar Series

  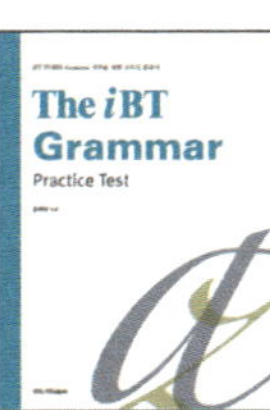

★★ **The iBT Grammar**
for Beginners / for All Learners / Practice Test

Winning TOEFL

Speaking Step

2 | **Answer Keys & Listening Script**

Step 3

Step 2

Step 1

Answer Keys & Listening Script

Answer Keys

Independent Task — Favorites Ⅰ

🔳 Key Expressions

Let's Practice

1. **My favorite music** is Jazz.
2. **First**, I like **hearing the sound of the saxophone**.
3. **Secondly**, I love to **listen to live music**.
4. **That's why** I like to **listen to Jazz**.

🔳 Practice

Get Started

1. strategies
2. competitive
3. tournament
4. patience
5. endurance

Speak Up (Sample answer)

My favorite (sport) / game is **soccer**. There are two reasons why **soccer** is my favorite. First, **I like to play sports with lots of people. We can develop team strategies because it is a multi-player sport**. Secondly, **I like to watch the World Cup. It is the biggest tournament in the world, and people from all over the world cheer for their countries all summer**. That's why my favorite (sport) / game is **soccer**.

🔳 Test (Sample answer)

My favorite subject in school is History. There are two reasons why History is my favorite subject. First, I love to learn about the lives of our ancestors. I like to put myself in the shoes of a historical person and imagine myself making the same discoveries and decisions. Secondly, it is important to know what has been done in the past. If we know what has been done before, we can find new ways to improve the future without repeating mistakes. That is why my favorite class is History.

Integrated Task — Problem Solving

🔳 Key Expressions

Let's Practice

The woman's problem is that she has a doctor's **appointment on the day of her field trip**. There are two possible solutions for this. **One is that** she could **tell her teacher that she can't go**. **The other is that** she could **ask her doctor to change the date**. I think **the first / second solution** is better.

🔳 Practice

Get Started

1. drop
2. fall behind
3. stressed out
4. harm
5. difficult
6. mistake

Get Ready

A-1

① stresses
② difficult
③ falling
④ behind
⑤ no
⑥ mistake
⑦ drop
⑧ GPA
⑨ taking
⑩ money
⑪ harm
⑫ hundred
⑬ help
⑭ professor
⑮ study
⑯ extra
⑰ busy
⑱ questions

A-2

1. Ⓐ   2. Ⓑ, Ⓒ

Speak Up ⠶ (Sample answer)

☑ Solution1   ☐ Solution2

The man's problem is that he finds it too difficult to keep up in Chemistry class. The woman suggests two possible solutions. One is that he could drop the course. The other is that he could get extra help from others. I think the first solution is better. First of all, he will risk failing the course. It will reflect poorly on his GPA. By dropping the course, he can then focus on his other courses and raise his GPA, rather than harm it. In addition, losing a hundred dollars is better than getting an F. If there is an F on his transcript, it will be difficult for him to go to a good school. For these reasons, I think the man should choose the first option.

☐ Solution1   ☑ Solution2

The man's problem is that he finds it too difficult to keep up in Chemistry class. The woman suggests two possible solutions. One is that he could drop the course. The other is that he could get extra help from others. I think the second solution is better. First of all, it is a waste of money to drop the class. A hundred dollars is a lot of money for students, but it won't cost any money to get into a study group or get extra help from the professor. In addition, a study group can be very helpful and effective. I'm sure he will improve if he gets help from others. They can help each other by comparing answers and discussing how they came to their conclusions. For these reasons, I think the man should choose the second option.

Test (Sample answer)

☑ Solution 1   ☐ Solution 2

The woman's problem is that she is having difficulty falling asleep these days. The man suggests two solutions. One is that she could get more exercise. The other is that she could go to see a therapist. In my opinion, the first option is better. First of all, exercising will make her healthier overall. Jogging or walking will help her sleep better and, at the same time, she will feel healthier. Therefore, even though she is very busy, she must make spare time to exercise. Second of all, she might feel embarrassed to see a therapist. Her classmates will make fun of her if they know that she goes to see a therapist. For these reasons, I think the woman should choose the first option.

☐ Solution 1   ☑ Solution 2

The woman's problem is that she is having trouble sleeping lately. The man suggests two solutions. One is that she could get more exercise. The other is that she could go to see a therapist. In my opinion, the second option is better. First, she doesn't even have time to exercise. It is faster to go and see a therapist and solve her sleeping problem immediately. Second, there is nothing wrong with seeing a therapist. It is so untrue that therapy is only for people with mental problems. These therapists are trained to help you cope with a variety of everyday issues. For these reasons, I think the woman should choose the second option.

Unit 2

Independent Task Favorites II

Key Expressions

Let's Practice ⠶

1. I would have to say that my favorite city is New York.

2. Nobody was there when I arrived.

3. I fall asleep when I watch movies at home.

4. The **first reason is that there are lots of museums and historical places to see** .

⌑ Practice

Get Started

1. stunt
2. brave
3. sweat
4. imaginary
5. kept me on the edge of my seat

Speak Up (Sample answer)

I would have to say that my favorite movie genre is **action**. There are two reasons why **action** is my favorite genre. The first reason is that **time flies when I watch action movies. Action movies are so exciting that they keep me on the edge of my seat** . The second reason is that **I like to watch actors or actresses perform stunts. They are so amazing** . That's why I like **action** movies.

⌑ Test (Sample answer)

I would have to say that the most meaningful object I have is my collector's edition baseball bat. There are two reasons why this baseball bat is the most meaningful object that I have. The first reason is that this bat reminds me of my grandmother. My grandmother gave it to me as a gift when I was a young boy. The second reason is that it is very rare and is worth a lot of money now. Over the years, this bat has become very hard to find. That is why my collector's edition baseball bat is the most meaningful object I have.

Integrated Task Problem Solving

⌑ Key Expressions

Let's Practice

1. She could **either go to bed early and wake up early or stay awake all night** .

2. If **she goes to bed late and gets up late** ,

she will **definitely miss the morning class** .

3. **Studying English** is **not that easy** .

⌑ Practice

Get Started

1. rest
2. on time
3. irresponsible
4. important
5. give up
6. concentrate

Get Ready

A-1

① party
② reading
③ assignment
④ tomorrow
⑤ irresponsible
⑥ lazy
⑦ give up
⑧ on
⑨ possible
⑩ best
⑪ important
⑫ rest
⑬ enjoy
⑭ call
⑮ concentrate

A-2

1. Ⓐ   2. Ⓒ, Ⓓ

Speak Up (Sample answer)

☑ Solution1   ☐ Solution2

The woman's problem is that **she has to finish some reading for her study group by tomorrow, but she wants to go to a party tonight** . The man gives her **two** possible solutions. She could either **give up the party and stay up late to finish the reading,** or she could **tell her study group members that she can't make it and just enjoy the party** . I think the **first** solution is much better. First, **breaking promises for a party shows that she is irresponsible. A study group is a form of group work. If she does not finish her part, it will have a negative effect on the others in the group. Then she will lose their trust** . Secondly, **there is a difference between not trying and not doing. If she could not finish the reading, other members would understand her. However, if they found out** she did not even try to finish the reading because of the party, they would be very upset**. These are the reasons that I think the **first** solution is better.

☐ Solution1   ☑ Solution2

The woman's problem is that **she has to finish some reading for her study group by tomorrow, but she wants to go to a party tonight**. The man gives her **two** possible solutions. She could either **give up the party and stay up late to finish the reading,** or she could **tell her study group members that she can't make it and just enjoy the party** . I think the **second** solution is much better. First, **it is impossible for her to finish the reading anyway. So she should just have fun instead** . Secondly, **it will be a waste of time doing the reading. It's because all she can think about is the party and will not be able to concentrate** . These are the reasons that I think the **second** solution is better.

🔲 Test (Sample answer)

☑ Solution 1   ☐ Solution 2

The man's problem is that he has to write a paper after visiting a museum, but he has no time to visit. The woman suggests two solutions to the problem. He could either skip his afternoon classes and visit the museum to write his paper, or he could ask for an extension. I think the first solution is better. First, the man can get class notes from his friend. If the man tells his friend the situation, his friend will give him all of the information. Secondly, asking for an extension will lower his grade. The man did not do so well on his midterm, and the professor is very strict about deadlines. So, it is better to hand the paper in on time. These are the reasons that I think the first solution is better.

☐ Solution 1   ☑ Solution 2

The man's problem is that he has to write a paper after visiting a museum, but he has no time to visit. The woman suggests two

solutions to the problem. He could either skip his afternoon classes and visit the museum to write his paper, or he could ask for an extension. I think the second solution is better. First, this class is the most important class before the final exam. If he doesn't attend, he may not get all of the information he needs. Especially after a bad midterm, it is important to attend all the classes. Secondly, it is better to write the paper thoroughly with an extension. Even if the professor is strict about deadlines, he will not give a good grade if the quality of the paper is poor. These are the reasons that the second solution is better.

Independent Task   Persons

🔲 Key Expressions

Let's **Practice** ⋮⋗

1. **The person** who is the funniest in my class is **Ross** .

2. **The person who is the most intelligent in my class** is **Crystal** .

3. **The person** who I like the most is **my mom** .

4. **The person who I care about the most** is **my nephew, Sam** .

🔲 Practice

Get **Started** ⋮⋗

①–ⓒ   ②–ⓓ   ③–ⓐ   ④–ⓔ   ⑤–ⓑ

Speak Up ⋮⋗ (Sample answer)

The person who is the most important to me is **my mother** . There are two reasons why he(she)is so important to me. First of all, **she** has always been supportive of me. When I fail, she encourages me to keep trying . Secondly, she has always been patient with me. She has given me the time I needed to realize my faults and fix them myself . (This has made me into the person I am today.) That's why my mother is the most important person to me.

🖵 Test (Sample answer)

The person who(m) I admire the most is my father. There are two reasons why I admire my father the most. First of all, he has sacrificed so much to provide for the family. My father is a doctor. He goes to work early in the morning and finishes late at night. Sometimes, he works on the weekend to support our family. Secondly, he has become successful because of his own hard work. Even when times were rough, my father earned his own money and went to school. Now, he is one of the most well-known doctors in the country. That's why I admire my father the most.

Integrated Task Summary

🖵 Key Expressions

Let's Practice :::

The main topic of the lecture is two types of personality . According to the professor , there is an introvert and an extrovert . The example the professor gives for an introvert is Anna . And, the professor discusses an extroverted personality using the example of Tracy .

🖵 Practice

Get Started :::

①-ⓓ ②-ⓐ ③-ⓔ ④-ⓑ ⑤-ⓕ ⑥-ⓒ

Get Ready :::

Ⓐ

① difficult   ② methods   ③ repetition
④ collect   ⑤ efficiently   ⑥ flashcards
⑦ over   ⑧ over   ⑨ link
⑩ eyes   ⑪ brains   ⑫ remember
⑬ senses   ⑭ connections
⑮ object   ⑯ language   ⑰ brain
⑱ apple   ⑲ say   ⑳ hear
㉑ write   ㉒ see   ㉓ taste

Ⓑ

① two   ② repetition   ③ information
④ students use flashcards to learn new vocabulary
⑤ link   ⑥ eyes   ⑦ brains
⑧ use all five senses   ⑨ connections
⑩ language   ⑪ brain
⑫ *pomme*: apple in French
⑬ say   ⑭ hear   ⑮ write
⑯ see   ⑰ taste

Ⓒ

1. F   2. F   3. T   4. F   5. T   6. T

Ⓓ

1. The main topic of this lecture is learning a new language .

2. According to the professor, there are two main methods for learning a new language; repetition and the use of all five senses .

3. The example the professor gives is students who use flashcards to learn new words .

4. By repeating the action of using flashcards, students can build a clear link between the eyes and the brain.

5. The example the professor gives is the word *pomme*, the French word for apple .

6. By using all five senses, students are able to make connections with the object, language and the brain .

Speak Up ⁙ (Sample answer)

The main topic of the lecture is learning a new language. According to the professor, there are two main methods for learning a new language: repetition and the use of all five senses. The professor discusses the first method in learning a new language which is repetition. The example she gives is students who use flashcards to learn new words. By repeating the action of using flashcards, students can build a clear link between the eyes and the brain. Then the professor talks about the second method which is using all five senses. The example she gives is the word *pomme*, the French word for apple. By using all five senses, students are able to make connections with the object, language, and the brain.

Test (Sample answer)

The main topic of the lecture is peer pressure. The professor explains that peer pressure is the influence of a peer group on an individual. According to him, there are two types of peer pressure: negative and positive. The professor discusses negative peer pressure using the example of Sean. He has a group of friends who skip class and don't study. He feels pressured to fit in with his group of friends by doing the same. Then the professor talks about positive peer pressure using the example of Joy. She hangs out with a group of studious and diligent friends. She feels that she must study hard in order to keep up with her friends.

Unit 4

Independent Task   Characteristics

Key Expressions

Let's Practice ⁙

As far as I'm concerned, learning other languages is difficult. In my opinion, English, especially, is the most difficult language to study. So, I should keep reading books and listening to the news. Also, I should practice speaking English frequently. That way, I will be able to improve my ability to speak English.

Practice

Get Started ⁙

①-ⓒ   ②-ⓔ   ③-ⓐ   ④-ⓕ   ⑤-ⓑ   ⑥-ⓓ

Speak Up ⁙ (Sample answer)

As far as I'm concerned, there are two important characteristics of a student leader. In my opinion, a student leader should be confident about his/her own abilities. Others will have the same beliefs and want to follow their leader if the leader has confidence in himself/herself. Also, a student leader must lead by example. A student leader must be able to act diligently and work harder than everyone else. So, he/she would be able to gain the respect of other students.

Test (Sample answer)

As far as I'm concerned, there are two important characteristics of a good neighbor. In my opinion, neighbors should be respectful. Neighbors can solve problems quickly if they respect each other. So, they would be able to understand each other and cooperate. Also, neighbors should help each other during hard times. As they help each other, they will learn more about one another. This will make the community happier.

Key Expressions

Let's Practice

The lecture is **mainly about taking a nap**. The professor **explains that there are advantages and disadvantages to taking a nap**. The professor **begins by** discussing some beneficial factors when taking a nap for a short time. **The professor uses Ally** who sleeps for 20 minutes after lunch **as an example**.

Practice

Get Started

1. fit into   2. complicated   3. solve

4. depth   5. measure   6. take off

Get Ready

A

① relate   ② tools   ③ ability

④ solve   ⑤ simple   ⑥ systematic

⑦ tools   ⑧ nature   ⑨ original

⑩ gorillas   ⑪ sticks   ⑫ measure

⑬ depth   ⑭ water   ⑮ complicated

⑯ humans   ⑰ shape   ⑱ changed

⑲ easier   ⑳ chimpanzees

㉑ remove   ㉒ leaves   ㉓ teeth

㉔ branches   ㉕ fit   ㉖ efficient

㉗ thinking

B

① animals   ② tools   ③ solve

④ problems   ⑤ original   ⑥ gorillas

⑦ sticks   ⑧ objects

⑨ measure depth of water

⑩ shape   ⑪ changed   ⑫ chimpanzees

⑬ leaves   ⑭ teeth   ⑮ branches

⑯ ant

C

1. T   2. F   3. T   4. T   5. T   6. F

7. T   8. F   9. F

D

1. The lecture is mainly about the **use of tools by animals**.

2. The professor explains that animals **have the ability to link objects to their everyday activities**.

3. According to the professor, some animals use tools in **simple ways** and some use them in **systematic ways**.

4. Simple tool use is when the animal uses **a tool in its original form**.

5. They use various objects such as sticks to **measure the depth of water**.

6. Systematic tool use is when the animal changes **the shape of an object to serve a specific function**.

7. They remove leaves from sticks and then **sharpen them with their teeth to fit into ant and termite nests**.

Speak Up (Sample answer)

The lecture is mainly about **the use of tools by animals**. The professor explains that **animals have the ability to link objects to their everyday activities**. According to the professor, **some animals use tools in simple ways and some use them in systematic ways**. He begins by introducing **the simple tool use**. This is **when the animal uses a tool in its original form**. The example he gives is **gorillas**. They use various objects such as sticks to **measure the depth of water**. The second type of tool use he explains is **systematic**. Systematic tool use is **when the animal changes the shape of an object to serve a specific function**. He uses **chimpanzees** as an example. They **remove leaves from sticks and then sharpen them with their teeth to fit into ant and termite nests**.

⊡ Test (Sample answer)

The lecture is mainly about species introduction and the different forms it commonly takes. The professor explains that species introduction is a process by which plants or animals are introduced to a new environment. According to the professor, there are two types of species introduction: intentional introduction and accidental introduction. She begins by introducing the first type of introduction, intentional. This is when a species of plant or animal is introduced to a new environment intentionally, usually for agricultural purposes. The example she gives is a Monterey pine tree. This tree is from California and now it is grown in Australia for timber purposes. The second type of species introduction she explains is accidental. This is when a species is introduced to a new environment unintentionally. She uses the zebra mussel as an example. It was brought over to America on the bottom of boats from Russia.

Unit 5

Independent Task   Preference

⊡ Key Expressions

Let's Practice

1. = I prefer to study alone rather than to study in a group .

   = I would choose to study alone .

2. = I prefer staying at home to going outside on weekends .

   = I would choose to stay at home on weekends .

⊡ Practice

Get Started

1. unique   2. experience   3. stains
4. rules   5. comfortable

Speak Up (Sample answer)

☑ **wear school uniforms**

☐ wear casual clothes

I prefer wearing school uniforms to wearing casual clothes . There are two reasons why I prefer wearing school uniforms . The first reason is that school uniforms take less time to prepare every morning. I never have to worry about what I'm going to wear, so I can get to school early . Another reason is that I don't have to spend money shopping for clothes. I can spend my money on other things, such as going to the movies and playing video games . That's why I would choose to wear school uniforms .

☐ wear school uniforms

☑ **wear casual clothes**

I prefer wearing casual clothes to wearing school uniforms . There are two reasons why I prefer wearing casual clothes . The first reason is that casual clothes are more comfortable. I don't like to wear skirts and ties. I feel far more comfortable wearing jeans and t-shirts . Another reason is that I like to look different from other people. I have my own style, and I like being unique and special . That's why I would choose to wear casual clothes .

⊡ Test (Sample answer)

☑ **eat lunch made by the school cafeteria**

☐ bring my own lunch

I prefer to eat lunch made by the school cafeteria rather than to bring my own lunch. There are two reasons why I prefer to eat the cafeteria's lunch. The first reason is that the food is freshly cooked. Because the food has just been cooked, students can enjoy the hot and fresh food. Another reason is that there are always different things on the menu. There is variety food to choose from, ranging from spaghetti to cheesecake. That's why I would choose to eat lunch made by the school cafeteria.

☐ eat lunch made by the school cafeteria
☑ bring my own lunch

I prefer to bring my own lunch rather than to eat lunch made by the school cafeteria. There are two reasons why I prefer to bring my own lunch. The first reason is that I can save money. If I bring my own lunch, I can save up to $100 a month. Another reason is that I don't have to waste time waiting in line. Instead, I can spend more time during the lunch break playing with my friends. That's why I would choose to bring my own lunch.

Integrated Task Fit & Explain

Key Expressions

Let's Practice

1. = **The man does not agree with the new proposal** .
   = **The man thinks that the new proposal is not a good idea** .
   = **The man is against the new proposal** .
   = **The man is opposed to the new proposal** .
2. = **The man is against raising the student union fee** .
   = **The man is opposed to raising the student union fee** .

Practice

Get Started

① – ⓒ ② – ⓔ ③ – ⓐ ④ – ⓖ ⑤ – ⓗ ⑥ – ⓑ
⑦ – ⓓ ⑧ – ⓕ ⑨ – ⓘ

Get Ready

A-1

The Recreation Center Committee proposed to have the student recreation center renovated and its facilities expanded due to poor facilities and large numbers of students using the center.

A-2

1. Ⓐ   2. Ⓐ, Ⓒ   3. Ⓐ
4. Ⓑ, Ⓒ   5. Ⓑ

B-1

① notice   ② expand   ③ remodel
④ time   ⑤ money   ⑥ swimming
⑦ facilities ⑧ line   ⑨ space
⑩ weekends   ⑪ busy   ⑫ pay
⑬ use   ⑭ June   ⑮ fair
⑯ seniors

B-2

1. Ⓑ   2. Ⓒ, Ⓓ

B-3

① time   ② money   ③ excellent
④ wait   ⑤ plenty   ⑥ seniors
⑦ three   ⑧ graduate

Speak Up (Sample answer)

The Recreational Center Committee is going to **remodel the student recreation center** because **the facilities are old and are inadequate** . The woman thinks the university's plan to renovate the student recreation center is **not a good idea** . There are two main reasons why she **disagrees** with the plan. First of all, she thinks **it is a big waste of time and money. She goes to the center regularly and thinks the facilities are excellent. Also, she has never had to wait in line because there is plenty of space on the weekdays** . Second of all, she thinks **it is unfair that seniors have to pay for the construction. Seniors have to pay for the construction, but can only use the center for three months because they** graduate in June next year. For these reasons, the woman **does not agree** with the idea.

Test (Sample answer)

The library is going to have a different schedule for the summer session. It is going to be closed in the evenings and on weekends. The man is opposed to this new library schedule. There are two main reasons why he thinks it's not a good idea. First of all, he thinks that it is unfair for students who are taking summer courses because they will not have access to the same facilities as students attending in spring and fall terms. This is especially unfair because summer students pay the same costs as spring and fall term students. Second of all, he thinks that students use the library mostly in the evenings and on weekends. So it's better to close in the morning since students are busy during the day. For these reasons, he is against the changes of the library hours.

Unit 6

Independent Task   Preference

Key Expressions

Let's Practice

1. = **I would rather live in the countryside than live in a city**.

   = **I think living in the countryside is better than living in a city**.

2. = **I like to go to a museum rather than to go to an amusement park**.

   = **I would rather go to a museum than go to an amusement park**.

Practice

Get Started

1. competitiveness   2. secluded

3. effectively   4. provoke

5. distractions

Speak Up (Sample answer)

☑ **study at home**

☐ **study in the library**

I like to study **at home** rather than to study **in the library**. There are two reasons why I think studying **at home** is better. The first reason is that **it is much more comfortable. I can sit on my bed and study in my pajamas, and I can take breaks whenever I want to**. Another reason is that **I have my own study style at home. I memorize things by saying them aloud repeatedly. I also walk around the house to clear my thoughts**. That's why I would rather study **at home** than study **in the library**.

☐ **study at home**

☑ **study in the library**

I like to study **in the library** rather than to study **at home**. There are two reasons why I think studying **in the library** is better. The first reason is that **I can concentrate deeply on my studies. I concentrate better in a secluded area where I can see lots of other students who are also studying hard**. Another reason is that **there are fewer distractions in the library. When I am at home, I always turn on the T.V., go on the internet, or talk on the phone with friends. Sometimes, I even fall asleep**. That's why I would rather study **in the library** than study **at home**.

Test (Sample answer)

☑ **take courses on campus**

☐ **take courses on-line**

I think taking courses on campus is better than taking courses on-line. There are two reasons why I like to take courses on campus. The first reason is that I can interact with other students. I like to meet new people in my classes and make new friends. It is good to make friends because they can help me when I feel sick and can't make it to class. Another reason is that I can understand things more easily. I like to talk with my instructor one-on-one. This way s/he can help me with things that I have difficulty understanding. That's why I would choose to take courses on campus.

☐ take courses on campus
☑ take courses on-line

I think taking courses on-line is better than taking courses on campus. There are two reasons why I like to take courses on-line. The first reason is that, I can watch lectures at any time. I can watch lectures at night if I get up late in the morning, or I can watch lectures in the morning if I am tired at night. Another reason is that I can watch lectures anywhere there is an internet connection. I like to go to my friend's house and watch lectures together. That's why I would choose to take courses on-line.

Integrated Task   Fit & Explain

🖵 Key Expressions

Let's Practice ⁘

1. = The man is for the new proposal.
   = The man thinks that the new proposal is a good idea.
2. = The man thinks it is a good idea to raise the student union fee.

🖵 Practice

Get Started ⁘

1. Ⓒ   2. Ⓑ   3. Ⓐ   4. Ⓒ   5. Ⓐ

Get Ready ⁘

A-1

Since students have to wait a long time for their turn to print, there will now be restrictions on the usage of paper for the printers in the computer lab.

A-2

1. Ⓑ   2. Ⓑ   3. Ⓐ   4. Ⓐ

B-1

① upset   ② exam   ③ freshmen
④ seniors   ⑤ privileges   ⑥ pay
⑦ libraries   ⑧ less   ⑨ crowded
⑩ malfunction   ⑪ wait
⑫ broke   ⑬ line   ⑭ expensive

B-2

1. Ⓑ   2. Ⓑ, Ⓒ

B-3

① seniors   ② freshmen
③ privileges   ④ computer lab
⑤ crowded   ⑥ printers
⑦ Internet cafés   ⑧ libraries

Speak Up ⁘ (Sample answer)

The university plans to limit the maximum amount of printing based on the student's year of study. The woman is for the university's plan. There are two reasons why she agrees with the plan. First, she understands that seniors have a heavier workload than freshmen. So, they should have the privileges. Second, the computer lab is always crowded and its printers often break down. So, she thinks it is better to print at alternative places like Internet cafés and libraries. For these reasons, the woman thinks that restricting the amount of paper per person according to their school year is a good idea.

🖵 Test (Sample answer)

The school has made a final decision to cut the music program in order to fund the physical education department. The man is for the decision the school has made. There are two reasons why he agrees with the decision. First, he feels it is most important for children to learn how to live healthy lifestyles. He thinks that learning how to live an active and healthy life is more useful than learning how to play an instrument. Second, he believes that sports are important as they boost the school's reputation. When the sports teams are successful, the school receives a lot of funding and can attract great students each year. For these reasons, the man thinks that it is a good idea to cut the music program in favor of physical education.

Unit 7

Independent Task Agree / Disagree

🔲 Key Expressions

Let's Practice

I agree with the opinion that advertising affects children in bad ways. Children may be influenced by false advertising . Also, they may buy things impulsively . For these reasons, I believe that advertising affects children in bad ways.

🔲 Practice

Get Started

① - ⓓ   ② - ⓕ   ③ - ⓑ   ④ - ⓐ   ⑤ - ⓒ   ⑥ - ⓔ

Speak Up (Sample answer)

☑ Agree   ☐ Disagree

I agree with the opinion that television only has negative effects on children. There are two reasons why I agree with that opinion.

First, TV takes time away from other activities such as reading and exercising. Without those activities, children will not be able to gather knowledge and stay healthy. Second, children may be influenced by violence and degrading images on TV. There are many inappropriate scenes for children. Parents often worry about this. For these reasons, I believe that television only has negative effects on children.

☐ Agree   ☑ Disagree

I disagree with the opinion that television only has negative effects on children. There are two reasons why I disagree with that opinion. First, TV can help broaden a child's knowledge base. Children may learn something on TV that they may never learn in the classroom. Second, TV also provides good educational programs and news. Educational programs provide a fun and active way of learning. So, children may become more creative and imaginative. For these reasons, I believe that television does not only have negative effects on children.

🔲 Test (Sample answer)

☑ Agree   ☐ Disagree

I agree with the opinion that parents should monitor what their children watch on TV. There are two reasons why I agree with that opinion. First, children have young minds. They are easily influenced by negative and violent images that they see on TV. So, parents should be aware of the negative images that are portrayed on TV. Second, children must learn what is right and wrong. Parents must teach children that the things on TV are unrealistic and often negative. For these reasons, I believe that parents should monitor what their children watch on TV.

☐ Agree   ☑ Disagree

I disagree with the opinion that parents should not monitor what their children watch on TV. There are two reasons why I disagree with that opinion. First, parents should encourage children to become self-reliant and independent decision makers. Children know what is right or wrong, so it is important for parents to allow their children to make the right decision. Second, parent supervision makes children more rebellious. Instead of worrying, they need to trust their children. This trust will motivate the children to choose the right programs. For these reasons, I believe that parents should not monitor what their children watch on TV.

Integrated Task   General / Specific

Key Expressions

Let's Practice

The professor first points out that self-respect is how much you 'like' yourself. The professor gives an example of Jesse who loves to ice skate even though she's not that good at it. The second point the professor makes is that self-esteem is how 'highly' you think about yourself. As an example, the professor talks about Jay who failed in the final round of the dance competition, but decides to work harder to achieve his goal in the next competition.

Practice

Get Started

1. close
2. arm-in-arm
3. invisible
4. tension
5. uncomfortable
6. density
7. allow
8. access

Get Ready

A-1

Personal space is an invisible boundary around a person. It is thought of as a person's own territory.

A-2

① an invisible boundary around a person
② person's own territory
③ discomfort
④ feel uneasy
⑤ intimacy
⑥ cultural standards

B-1

① uncomfortable
② entered
③ personal space
④ intimacy
⑤ close
⑥ allow
⑦ access
⑧ tension
⑨ cultural standards
⑩ Korea
⑪ India
⑫ less
⑬ lower
⑭ density
⑮ America
⑯ Canada
⑰ three
⑱ four
⑲ arm-in-arm

B-2

① intimacy ② close ③ romantic
④ personal space ⑤ met
⑥ tension ⑦ cultural standards
⑧ densely ⑨ Korea ⑩ India
⑪ lower ⑫ America ⑬ Canada
⑭ walk with 3 to 4 inches separating them from each other
⑮ walk arm-in-arm

C

1. Ⓑ   2. Ⓐ

3. intimacy, cultural standards

D

1. T   2. F   3. F   4. T   5. T
6. T   7. T

Speak Up (Sample answer)

The lecture is mainly about personal space. Personal space is known as one's own personal territory. According to the professor, personal space depends on two factors: intimacy and cultural standards. The professor first points out that intimacy is the closeness one person feels to another person. She gives an example of romantic relationships where people allow each other to enter their personal space. The second point she makes is about cultural standards. Cultural standards also influence how much personal space a person needs. As an example of cultural standards, she talks about population density. In low-density places like America, people usually keep a distance when walking with friends. In high-density places like Korea, girls often link arms with their friends.

Test (Sample answer)

The lecture is mainly about the relationship between verbal and nonverbal signals. According to the professor, verbal signals are messages with words and nonverbal signals are wordless messages. The professor first points out that verbal and nonverbal signals usually show the same meaning. He gives an example of a time when he told his daughter that he loved her while smiling at her and giving her a kiss on her cheek. The second point he makes is that verbal and nonverbal signals can sometimes show conflicting meanings. As an example of conflicting meanings, he talks about a time when he and his son were making a tree house and his son accidentally hit him with a hammer. Although the professor told his son that he was not in pain, he had a pained expression on his face while he was speaking.

Independent Task Agree / Disagree

Key Expressions

Let's Practice

I believe that aliens exist. One of the reasons is that many people say that they have actually seen UFOs. For example, my father saw a UFO, when he was driving. The other reason is that mysterious things happen around us quite a bit. For instance, a huge sign in the backyard can't be explained by saying that a human did it overnight.

Practice

Get Started

①-ⓒ ②-ⓔ ③-ⓐ ④-ⓑ ⑤-ⓕ ⑥-ⓓ

Speak Up (Sample answer)

☑ Agree   ☐ Disagree

I believe that people behave differently depending on what type of clothing they wear. There are two reasons why I believe this. One of the reasons is that looks have an effect on how people act. For example, when I wear baggy clothes, like hip-hop artists, I speak like rappers and walk differently. The other reason is that people tend to treat a person differently depending upon the type of clothing they wear. For instance, when I wear a nice suit, people seem to treat me with a lot of respect. In response, I also treat the other people politely. That's why I agree that people behave differently depending on what type of clothing they wear.

☐ Agree   ☑ Disagree

I believe that people do not behave differently depending on what type of clothing they

wear . There are two reasons why I believe this. One of the reasons is that clothes themselves do not affect the way people act. People act differently because they feel different, not because of their clothes . The other reason is that most people do not care about what others think. For instance, I can walk right into a party wearing either a suit or sweat pants without a change in my behavior. My behavior does not change because of what I am wearing . That's why I **disagree** that people behave differently depending on what type of clothing they wear.

🔲 Test (Sample answer)

☑ **possible to know**

☐ **impossible to know**

I believe that it is possible to know a person's character based on a first impression. There are two reasons why I believe this. One of the reasons is that I can usually tell people's personalities by their appearance. For example, shy people tend to show up quietly and active people tend to appear very loud. The other reason is that it is hard to completely change who you are, even if only for a brief introduction. For instance, rude people may sound a bit hostile and nice people will sound more pleasant when they introduce themselves. That's why I agree that it is possible to know a person's character based on a first impression.

☐ **possible to know**

☑ **impossible to know**

I believe that it is impossible to know a person's character based on a first impression. There are two reasons why I believe this. One of the reasons is that a first impression depends mainly on external looks. Like it or not, people are born with their looks. For example, a person who has a scar from an accident can be judged as a violent or scary person. The other reason is that some people act differently when they first meet new people. For instance, some people might look cold and unfriendly upon first meeting them because they are shy. But, they may turn out to be very open-minded and friendly people when people get to know them well. That's why I disagree that it is possible to know a person's character based on a first impression.

Integrated Task General / Specific

🔲 Key Expressions

Let's Practice ⋰

1. I've changed my personality by **attending** social gatherings.
2. We enjoy **talking about** our old school days when we meet.
3. I gave up **being** cruel to my younger brother.
4. If you want somebody else to believe you, then you need to **believe in yourself** first.
5. When you feel so exhausted, you definitely need to **have time to yourself** .

🔲 Practice

Get Started ⋰

①-ⓙ ②-ⓘ ③-ⓓ ④-ⓐ ⑤-ⓛ ⑥-ⓖ
⑦-ⓕ ⑧-ⓑ ⑨-ⓚ ⑩-ⓒ ⑪-ⓗ ⑫-ⓔ

Get Ready ⋰

A-1

Generally speaking, people can be divided into two common personality types: introverts and extroverts.

A-2

① introverted   ② shy
③ outgoing   ④ new social contacts
⑤ extroverted   ⑥ energetic
⑦ adventurous

⑧ restore their energy through deep thought

⑨ find comfort in being around other people and tend to release energy

B-1

① introverted
② extroverted
③ stress
④ shy
⑤ outgoing
⑥ alone
⑦ stressed out
⑧ alone
⑨ think
⑩ reflect
⑪ thoughts
⑫ secure
⑬ relaxed
⑭ herself
⑮ sociable
⑯ others
⑰ out
⑱ large
⑲ basketball
⑳ parties
㉑ comforting

B-2

① introverts ② alone ③ space

④ likes to stay home, read books, take baths, have time to reflect on her own thoughts, feels secure & relaxed when she has time to herself

⑤ extroverts ⑥ sociable ⑦ go out

⑧ enjoys hanging out with friends, being in large groups, playing basketball & going to parties, finds it more comforting & enjoyable to be around others

C

1. Ⓐ

2. **Introverted personality type**
shy
reserved
less outgoing
have fewer friends
restore their energy through deep thought
like to be alone

Extroverted personality type
social
confident
adventurous
release energy
like to be in groups of people

D

1. F   2. T   3. T   4. F   5. F   6. T

Speak Up (Sample answer)

The lecture is mainly about introverted and extroverted personality types, and the different ways that people who fit into these types handle stress. According to the professor, introverted people like to get rid of stress by spending time alone. He uses the example of his friend, Crystal, to talk about the introverted personality type. Crystal usually relieves stress by doing things alone such as reading books and meditating. He then talks about the way extroverted people like to relieve stress by going outside and hanging out with people. As an example of the extroverted personality type, he tells us about Charles. Charles relieves stress by playing basketball and hanging out with his friends at parties.

Test (Sample answer)

The lecture is mainly about self-esteem. The professor discusses the difference between people with high self-esteem and low self-esteem. According to the professor, people with high self-esteem are more confident in their own abilities and put things into action as they believe. She uses the example of Jack. Jack failed to make the basketball team, but did not give up. Because he believed in himself and kept trying, Jack eventually became the team captain. She then talks about people with low self-esteem. They tend to give up easily and don't like challenges. As an example of a person with low self-esteem, she tells us about Tyler. When he did not make the ice hockey team, Tyler told himself he could never become a hockey player and gave up trying.

Question 1 of 6

As far as I'm concerned, there are two characteristics of a good group member. In my opinion, a good group member should always be a hard worker. A hard worker is necessary because if a problem arises, then someone must be willing to put in the extra effort to make sure things get done. For example, a group member may get sick or have a family emergency. Then the other group members must be willing to work hard to take on the missing member's work. Another trait a good group member should have is that they should be punctual. A punctual group member always makes sure he or she has things done on time and when it is needed. If things are not done on time, then it puts everyone behind schedule.

Question 2 of 6

☑ like discussion courses
☐ like lecture courses

I prefer discussion courses in small classrooms. There are two reasons why I think discussion courses in small classrooms are better. One reason is that there is more individual attention for each student. The students will then learn about the subject in more depth. It also forces students to actively participate. Another reason is that small classrooms allow you to become closer to your classmates and teacher. People are more social and develop deeper friendships. That's why I think discussion courses in small classrooms are better than lecture courses in large classrooms.

☐ like discussion courses
☑ like lecture courses

I prefer lecture courses in large classrooms.

There are two reasons why I think lecture courses in large classrooms are better. One reason is that there are more students in large classrooms and I get to meet more people. I have more choices on who I would like to study with. Another reason is that the atmosphere in large classrooms is more relaxed. People who are shy can learn more comfortably. When they receive lots of attention from the instructor, they become very nervous. That's why I think lecture courses in large classrooms are better than discussion courses in small classrooms.

Question 3 of 6

The Housing Committee has announced a plan to remove all TVs from the common areas of the dormitory. The committee is going to replace them with one large TV in the main lounge. The man is against the removal of the TVs from the common rooms. There are two reasons for this. First, he thinks that the main lounge is too far away, while the common rooms are close and convenient. Second, he feels that there are plenty of places to study other than the common room. He believes that students should not use the common room for studying because that is where people meet friends and relax. The library is much better for studying because it is quieter.

Question 4 of 6

The lecture is mainly about the different personalities of first-born children and last-born children. According to the professor, the personality of a person sometimes depends on the order in which they were born. The professor first talks about the personality traits of first-born children. First-born children usually have the personalities of perfectionists. He gives the example of his oldest son, Steve. Steve always acts like a grown up and feels responsible for taking care of house chores. The professor then talks about the personality traits of last-born children. Last-born children usually have adventurous and outgoing personalities. The example he gives is his youngest son, Ted. Ted likes to explore places and find new things.

☑ **Solution 1**

☐ **Solution 2**

The woman's problem is that she is trying to study for her exams, but her roommate is being too loud. The man suggests two possible solutions. One is that she should speak with her roommate directly. The other is that she should ask the resident advisor for a room change. I think the first solution is better. First, it is always better to speak in-person when you have a problem. This will prevent most misunderstandings from happening. It is also a sign of respect. Second, the school might not have any rooms available for her since it is in the middle of the school year. She also has to deal with packing and moving with exams coming up. This could be a large burden during such a stressful time. These are the reasons that I think the first solution is better.

☐ **Solution 1**

☑ **Solution 2**

The woman's problem is that she is trying to study for her exams, but her roommate is being too loud. The man suggests two possible solutions. One is that she should speak with her roommate directly. The other is that she should ask the resident advisor for a room change. I think the second solution is better. First, sometimes, the best way to solve a problem is to walk away. Confronting someone directly is not always the best way to solve a problem. This can sometimes lead to a serious argument or a fight with her roommate. Second, changing a room might work out better for both people. The girl will get a roommate who doesn't sing all the time, and her current roommate might be able to be placed with another music student. This way they can both focus more on their studies without having to worry about somebody else. These are the reasons that I think the second solution is better.

The lecture is mainly about long-term memory. The professor explains that long-term memory allows people to remember things for a long time. According to the lecture, there are two types of long-term memory: declarative and procedural. First, she discusses declarative memory, using the example of memorizing the order of colors in a rainbow. Using the mnemonic device, "Roy G. Biv," one can memorize the colors quickly and easily. As long as you use this mnemonic device, you will never forget the order of the colors. She then talks about procedural memory. Using the example of learning how to ride a bicycle, she explains that practice helps one learn through a process. This is different from declarative memory because procedural memory is about experience.

Listening Script

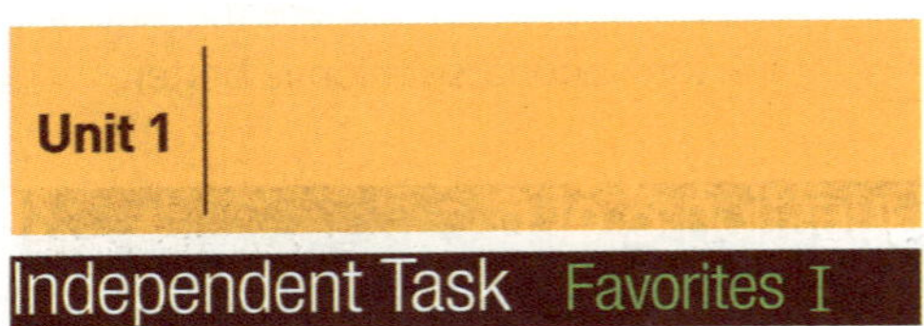

Unit 1

Independent Task   Favorites I

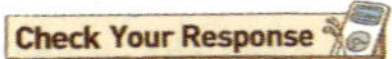 Practice

Speak Up

Check Your Response

My favorite sport is soccer. There are two reasons why soccer is my favorite. First, I like to play sports with lots of people. We can develop team strategies because it is a multi-player sport. Secondly, I like to watch the World Cup. It is the biggest tournament in the world, and people from all over the world cheer for their countries all summer. That's why my favorite sport is soccer.

Integrated Task   Problem Solving

Practice

Get Ready   A-1   B-1

W: Hey, you look really stressed out! What's going on?

M: Oh... It's this Chemistry class that stresses me out. It's too difficult for me. It's only the second week and I'm already falling behind.

W: Is it really that bad?

M: Yes! I have no idea what's going on. I think it was a mistake to take this course. What am I going to do?

W: Well, you could drop the course. If you think of your GPA, it's better not to keep taking it. You'll lose a bit of money, but it's better than getting a low grade. That will harm your GPA.

M: Yeah. I've thought of that. The problem is

that I'll end up losing about a hundred dollars. That's not a small amount of money.

W: Hmm... Then, how about this? Get some help from others. You could get extra help from the professor, or join a study group. There are many ways of getting extra help.

M: I thought about it, but I don't know many people, and the professor seems very busy.

W: I'm sure your professor would be happy to answer your questions.

Speak Up

Check Your Response

☑ Solution 1   ☐ Solution 2

The man's problem is that he finds it too difficult to keep up in Chemistry class. The woman suggests two possible solutions. One is that he could drop the course. The other is that he could get extra help from others. I think the first solution is better. First of all, he will risk failing the course. It will reflect poorly on his GPA. By dropping the course, he can then focus on his other courses and raise his GPA, rather than harm it. In addition, losing a hundred dollars is better than getting an F. If there is an F on his transcript, it will be difficult for him to go to a good school. For these reasons, I think the man should choose the first option.

☐ Solution 1   ☑ Solution 2

The man's problem is that he finds it too difficult to keep up in Chemistry class. The woman suggests two possible solutions. One is that he could drop the course. The other is that he could get extra help from others. I think the second solution is better. First of all, it is a waste of money to drop the class. A hundred dollars is a lot of money for students, but it won't cost any money to get into a study group or get extra help from the professor. In addition, a study group can be very helpful and effective. I'm sure he will improve if he gets help from others. They can help each other by comparing answers and discussing how they came to their conclusions. For these reasons, I think the man should choose the second option.

Test

A

W: Ugh. I'm so tired.

M: Yeah, you don't look so good today. What's wrong?

W: I don't know. I haven't been sleeping well lately. I go to bed at 11 or 12, but I just lie awake until 4 in the morning.

M: Hmm. Maybe you need to get more exercise. Sometimes, people can't sleep because they aren't active enough. You might think about jogging or going for a walk daily.

W: That's a good idea, but I'm not sure whether I really have time for that. I spend my whole day at school and then I do after-school activities.

M: In that case, what do you think about going to see a therapist?

W: A therapist? What do you mean?

M: I mean you could find someone to talk to about what's bothering you. Your problem might be stress-related. If you talk to a therapist and find out what is bothering you, you might sleep better. They can also provide sleep medication.

W: I feel kind of funny going to see a therapist. Hmm... I will have to think about it.

M: Why? Are you worried that people might think you're weird?

W: Actually, kind of. Isn't therapy only for people who have mental problems?

M: That's not true, it's a big misconception. Many normal people have to see therapists for everyday stress.

Unit 2

Independent Task Favorites II

Practice

Speak Up

Check Your Response

I would have to say that my favorite movie genre is action. There are two reasons why action is my favorite genre. The first reason is that time flies when I watch action movies. Action movies are so exciting that they keep me on the edge of my seat. The second reason is that I like to watch actors or actresses perform stunts. They are so amazing. That's why I like action movies.

Integrated Task Problem Solving

Practice

Get Ready A-1 B-1

M: Are you coming to the party tonight?

W: I really want to, but I'm not sure yet.

M: Why? What's wrong?

W: I'm in this study group, and there's a reading assignment that I have to do by tomorrow. There's no way I can finish it all by tomorrow anyway. If I don't finish the reading, they're going to think I'm irresponsible and lazy.

M: I bet that if you just give up the party and really work hard, you might get it done on time.

W: Hmm... But I don't think that's going to be possible. It's really too much.

M: I don't think your group members will think you are irresponsible if you try your best. Why don't you do the ones that are most important first? And then, if you have time, you can do the rest.

W: Yeah... I'm trying, but I'm not sure. Right now, all I can think about is the party.

M: Well... If you can't get it done either way, why don't you just enjoy yourself? Call the people in your study group and tell them that you won't be able to do it, and just come to the party! I don't think you'll be able to concentrate well anyways.

W: Yeah, but I don't think they'll be happy about it.

M: Of course they won't be too happy about it, but at least you can have fun and get a good night's sleep.

Speak Up

Check Your Response

☑ **Solution 1**   ☐ **Solution 2**

The woman's problem is that she has to finish some reading for her study group by tomorrow, but she wants to go to a party tonight. The man gives her two possible solutions. She could either give up the party and stay up late to finish the reading, or she could tell her study group members that she can't make it and just enjoy the party. I think the first solution is much better. First, breaking promises for a party shows that she is irresponsible. A study group is a form of group work. If she does not finish her part, it will have a negative effect on the others in the group. Then she will lose their trust. Secondly, there is a difference between not trying and not doing. If she could not finish the reading, other members would understand her. However, if they found out she did not even try to finish the reading because of the party, they would be very upset. These are the reasons that I think the first solution is better.

☐ **Solution 1**   ☑ **Solution 2**

The woman's problem is that she has to finish some reading for her study group by tomorrow, but she wants to go to a party tonight. The man gives her two possible solutions. She could either give up the party and stay up late to finish the reading, or she could tell her study group members that she can't make it and just enjoy the party. I think the second solution is much better. First, it is impossible for her to finish the reading anyway. So she should just have fun instead. Secondly, it will be a waste of time doing the reading. It's because all she can think about is the party and will not be able to concentrate. These are the reasons that I think the second solution is better.

Test

A

W: Is something wrong? You don't look so good.

M: I have to hand in this History paper, but I haven't even been to the museum yet. Above all, I have no time.

W: Do you have to go the museum to write the paper?

M: Yes, and the problem is that it's due Monday!

W: Well, you can still go today, tomorrow, or Sunday.

M: I can't. I have too many classes today. Tomorrow is a public holiday, so it's closed, and it's always closed on Sundays.

W: Ugh, why haven't you gone already?

M: Well, I have been busy all week and I had lots of homework. I guess I forgot.

W: Okay, here is what you can do. You can just skip today's afternoon classes and go to the museum.

M: I can't really do that because my afternoon classes are for my major. Besides, I have a test next week and the professor might talk about it.

W: Is it going to be a big test or just a quiz?

M: This is quite a big test before the final exam. And I almost failed my last midterm, so I really need to get a good grade on this.

W: Then, have you asked the professor for an extension?

M: I don't know if that's possible. Professor Smith is famous for having strict due dates. I think he will take some points off if I hand it in late.

Independent Task   Persons

🖳 Practice

Speak Up ⋮⋮

Check Your Response 📟

The person who is the most important to me is my mother. There are two reasons why she is so important to me. First of all, she has always been supportive of me. When I fail, she encourages me to keep trying. Secondly, she has always been patient with me. She has given me the time I needed to realize my faults and fix them myself. This has made me into the person I am today. That's why my mother is the most important person to me.

Integrated Task   Summary

🖳 Practice

Get Ready Ⓐ Ⓑ ⋮⋮

Professor: I believe that everyone already knows that learning a new language is a very difficult process. When learning a new language, there are two main methods that help many students learn faster. The first method is repetition. Through repetition, people can collect information faster and more efficiently. An example of this is when students use flashcards to learn new vocabulary. Through the repetition of seeing the same word and defining it over and over, they build a clear link between their eyes and brains to help remember new words. The second method in learning a new language is to use all five senses. When something is being used through all five senses, they are making multiple connections with the object, language, and the brain. An example can be seen in the word *pomme*, which means apple in French. To learn this word, an apple must now be referred to as a *pomme*. They must now say the word, hear the word, write the word, see the object, and taste the object in order to remember *pomme*.

Speak Up ⋮⋮

Check Your Response 📟

The main topic of the lecture is learning a new language. According to the professor, there are two main methods for learning a new language: repetition and the use of all five senses. The professor discusses the first method in learning a new language which is repetition. The example she gives is students who use flashcards to learn new words. By repeating the action of using flashcards, students can build a clear link between the eyes and the brain. Then the professor talks about the second method which is using all five senses. The example she gives is the word *pomme*, the French word for apple. By using all five senses, students are able to make connections with the object, language, and the brain.

🖳 Test

Ⓐ

Professor: Have you ever been pressured by your friends into doing something that you didn't want to do? Everyday we deal with peer pressure. Peer pressure is the influence of a peer group on an individual. These influences drive us to change our opinions, attitudes, or behavior in order to fit into a certain group. A peer group can be friends or even family. There is a lot of negative peer pressure in the world today. Adolescents, and even adults, deal with negative peer pressure about things such as smoking, drinking alcohol and shoplifting. It can be something as small as skipping class, or even staying out too late. A negative example of peer pressure can be seen in the case of Sean. Sean has a group of friends who don't study much and often skip class to play. Sean feels pressured to do the same in order to fit in with the group. However, peer pressure is not always negative. There are times when our friends try to pressure us to do something positive, such as to study for an upcoming exam. Joy is a good example of someone with positive peer pressure in her life. She has a group of friends who are the opposite of Sean's friends. Joy's friends often form study groups and work hard for their grades. She also puts a lot of effort to fit in with her peer group.

Unit 4

Independent Task Characteristics

[•••] Practice

Speak **U**p

Check Your Response

As far as I'm concerned, there are two important characteristics of a student leader. In my opinion, a student leader should be confident about his own abilities. Others will have the same beliefs and want to follow their leader if the leader has confidence in himself. Also, a student leader must lead by example. A student leader must be able to act diligently and work harder than everyone else. So, he would be able to gain the respect of other students.

Integrated Task Summary

[•••] Practice

Get **R**eady Ⓐ Ⓑ

Professor: Did you know that animals are able to relate the use of tools to everyday activities? This shows that animals have an advanced ability to solve problems. There are two different ways animals use tools: simple ways and systematic ways. The simple use of tools is when animals use tools or things in nature in their original form. An example of the simple tool use comes from gorillas. Gorillas use sticks and other long objects in nature to measure the depth of water. Then what is the systematic tool use? This is a more complicated technique, and it is similar to techniques used by humans. It is when a shape or appearance of an object is changed to make work easier. An example of this can be seen in chimpanzees. Chimpanzees remove leaves from branches and then sharpen them with their teeth. Chimpanzees use these sharp branches to fit into ant and termite nests. Using these tools, chimpanzees make their work more efficient. This shows that they are more advanced in their thinking.

Speak **U**p

Check Your Response

The lecture is mainly about the use of tools by animals. The professor explains that animals have the ability to link objects to their everyday activities. According to the professor, some animals use tools in simple ways and some use them in systematic ways. He begins by introducing the simple tool use. This is when the animal uses a tool in its original form. The example he gives is gorillas. They use various objects such as sticks to measure the depth of water. The second type of tool use he explains is systematic. Systematic tool use is when the animal changes the shape of an object to serve a specific function. He uses chimpanzees as an example. They remove leaves from sticks and then sharpen them with their teeth to fit into ant and termite nests.

[•••] Test

Ⓐ

Professor: Does anyone know what a Monterey pine tree is? It is a tree found in Monterey, California. But, that is now being grown in Australia as well. So, what brings the Monterey Pine to Australia? The Australian Monterey pine is an example of species introduction, a process through which a plant or animal is either intentionally or accidentally introduced to a new environment. In the case of intentional introduction, a species is purposely brought to a new area by humans. This type of introduced species is not intended to harm the environment. In fact, the introduction is usually done for agricultural purposes. Intentional species introduction often happens because a grower wants to produce a certain crop found in other parts of the world. An example of this is the Monterey pine, which is grown in Australia for timber purposes. The other type of species introduction is accidental. Accidental species introduction happens when a species is transported to a new place by human vectors such as ships. This type of introduction usually causes damage. An example of this is the zebra mussel, a species that was brought from Russia to North America on the bottom of boats.

Unit 5

Independent Task Preference

▣ Practice

Speak Up ⋙

Check Your Response

- ☑ **wear school uniforms**
- ☐ **wear casual clothes**

I prefer wearing school uniforms to wearing casual clothes. There are two reasons why I prefer wearing school uniforms. The first reason is that school uniforms take less time to prepare every morning. I never have to worry about what I'm going to wear, so I can get to school early. Another reason is that I don't have to spend money shopping for clothes. I can spend my money on other things, such as going to the movies and playing video games. That's why I would choose to wear school uniforms.

- ☐ **wear school uniforms**
- ☑ **wear casual clothes**

I prefer wearing casual clothes to wearing school uniforms. There are two reasons why I prefer wearing casual clothes. The first reason is that casual clothes are more comfortable. I don't like to wear skirts and ties. I feel far more comfortable wearing jeans and t-shirts. Another reason is that I like to look different from other people. I have my own style, and I like being unique and special. That's why I would choose to wear casual clothes.

Integrated Task Fit & Explain

▣ Practice

Get Ready B-1 B-3 ⋙

W: Did you see the notice about the recreation center?

M: No. What's it about?

W: They're going to expand the recreation center!

M: Well, I think it's a great idea! The basketball court we're using now is terrible. The locker rooms are particularly bad. It's about time they remodel that place.

W: Do you really think so? I think it's a big waste of time and money. I go to the recreation center regularly to use the fitness center and swimming pool. I think the facilities are excellent and I've never had to wait in line. They have plenty of space.

M: That's strange. I had to wait for at least an hour whenever I wanted to use a badminton court.

W: Well, perhaps only Fridays and weekends are busy. Besides, do you know that we have to pay for the new recreation center? We can't use it much anyway, because we are graduating in June next year. I don't think that's fair to seniors.

Speak Up

The Recreational Center Committee is going to remodel the student recreation center because the facilities are old and are inadequate. The woman thinks the university's plan to renovate the student recreation center is not a good idea. There are two main reasons why she disagrees with the plan. First of all, she thinks it is a big waste of time and money. She goes to the center regularly and thinks the facilities are excellent. Also, she has never had to wait in line because there is plenty of space on the weekdays. Second of all, she thinks it is unfair that seniors have to pay for the construction. Seniors have to pay for the construction, but can only use the center for three months because they graduate in June next year. For these reasons, the woman does not agree with the idea.

Test

M: Did you see the notice about the summer library schedule?

W: Yes, I did.

M: I think it's unfair for students who are taking summer courses.

W: Yes, but most of the part-time staff are students, so they probably aren't around in the summer. I guess the school is just trying to save money by reducing the hours so the full-time staff don't have to work overtime.

M: But, from the students' point of view, summer courses cost just as much as courses in the spring and fall terms. That means they are paying the same amount, but aren't getting the same services in the summer. It's so unfair.

W: There aren't that many students who take courses in the summer session anyway.

M: Oh, you'd be surprised. My classes for the summer session are already full. Also, most students are busy during the daytime. So, we usually study in the evenings and on weekends. It doesn't make sense to close the library at those times. If they wanted to reduce the hours, why couldn't they close the library in the morning instead?

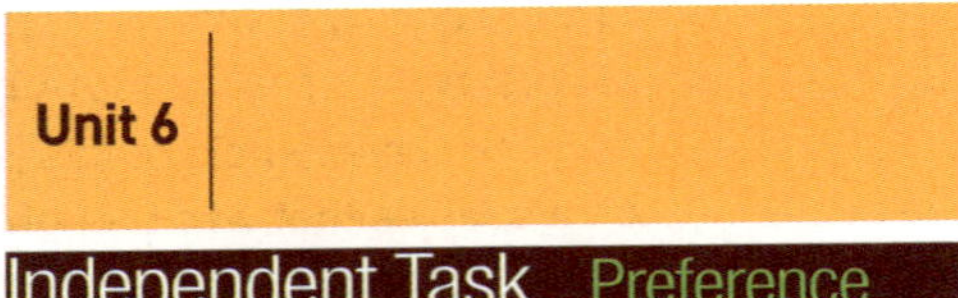

Unit 6

Independent Task Preference

Practice

Speak Up

☑ **study at home**

☐ **study in the library**

I like to study at home rather than to study in the library. There are two reasons why I think studying at home is better. The first reason is that it is much more comfortable. I can sit on my bed and study in my pajamas, and I can take breaks whenever I want to. Another reason is that I have my own study style at home. I memorize things by saying them aloud repeatedly. I also walk around the house to clear my thoughts. That's why I would rather study at home than study in the library.

□ study at home

☑ study in the library

I like to study in the library rather than to study at home. There are two reasons why I think studying in the library is better. The first reason is that I can concentrate deeply on my studies. I concentrate better in a secluded area where I can see lots of other students who are also studying hard. Another reason is that there are fewer distractions in the library. When I am at home, I always turn on the T.V., go on the internet, or talk on the phone with friends. Sometimes, I even fall asleep. That's why I would rather study in the library than study at home.

Integrated Task   Fit & Explain

Practice

Get Ready B-1 B-3

M: Hey, did you happen to see the notice about printing paper in the computer lab?

W: Yes, I did. You seem quite upset about it. It's only for the exam period, isn't it?

M: I just think it's unfair for freshmen. I think we should have the same right as the seniors.

W: Yes, but it's true that seniors have a lot more to print than us. They have to print more because they have to write longer essays. It makes sense that they should get the privileges.

M: Well, I usually print out my lecture notes to help me study, but now we have to pay for it at some internet cafés or libraries. That is going to be so expensive.

W: Yes, but internet cafés and libraries are less crowded. The computer lab may have been free, but do you remember what happened last exam period?

M: No. What happened?

W: It was so crowded! The printers began to malfunction and you had to wait at least 30 minutes just to print a few pages. Plus, I remember one time when the printers broke down and I had to wait in line for 20 minutes. I didn't get to print anything!

M: Yeah, I do remember that. I guess it's just that I'm used to it being free.

W: It's not too expensive. I'd rather pay the extra 50 cents.

Speak Up

 Check Your Response

The university plans to limit the maximum amount of printing based on the student's year of study. The woman is for the university's plan. There are two reasons why she agrees with the plan. First, she understands that seniors have a heavier workload than freshmen. So, they should have the privileges. Second, the computer lab is always crowded and its printers often break down. So, she thinks it is better to print at alternative places like internet cafés and libraries. For these reasons, the woman thinks that restricting the amount of paper per person according to their school year is a good idea.

Test

B

W: Can you believe that the committee would just cut the music program that easily?

M: Yeah, but you have to understand that our school's financial situation is not that great. We can't forget that.

W: Yeah... well, I still think it's unfair how they cut every component of the music program.

M: But don't you agree that students are getting fat and lazy because they don't get enough exercise? I would rather have physical education class than music class. Students should learn how to live active and healthy lifestyles rather than how to play an instrument.

W: Well, I think music is important as well. People say that when you play an instrument you become smarter.

M: That's true, but I still believe sports play a larger role in school spirit. It's because of those sports teams that our school is well-known. We can attract great students with our reputation. There is no way the committee will ever end sports programs.

W: Yeah, but our music program is great too. Lots of students participate in it.

M: Well...I think that music is something we can do as an extra-curricular activity after school.

Unit 7

Independent Task   Agree / Disagree

Practice

Speak Up

Check Your Response

☑ Agree   ☐ Disagree

I agree with the opinion that television only has negative effects on children. There are two reasons why I agree with that opinion. First, TV takes time away from other activities such as reading and exercising. Without those activities, children will not be able to gather knowledge and stay healthy. Second, children may be influenced by violence and degrading images on TV. There are many inappropriate scenes for children. Parents often worry about this. For these reasons, I believe that television only has negative effects on children.

☐ Agree   ☑ Disagree

I disagree with the opinion that television only has negative effects on children. There are two reasons why I disagree with that opinion. First, TV can help broaden a child's knowledge base. Children may learn something on TV that they may never learn in the classroom. Second, TV also provides good educational programs and news. Educational programs provide a fun and active way of learning. So, children may become more creative and imaginative. For these reasons, I believe that television does not only have negative effects on children.

Integrated Task   General / Specific

Practice

Get Ready   B-1   B-2

Professor: So, I guess we have all been in that awkward situation where someone is standing too close to us. We feel uncomfortable because somebody has entered our personal boundary. This boundary is often referred to as our personal space. Personal space gets wider or narrower depending on two factors. The first is intimacy. The degree of intimacy we feel towards people determines how close we allow them to get to us. For example, when two people are in a romantic relationship, they each allow the other access to this personal space. However, when two people have just met, and one person comes very close to the other person's face, it creates a strange tension. Another factor is cultural standards. People from densely populated areas, such as Korea or India, require less personal space than people from countries with a lower population density, such as America or Canada. Have you noticed that American people often walk with three to four inches separating them from each other, even though they are best friends? On the other hand, Korean girls like to walk arm-in-arm if they are close friends.

Check Your Response

The lecture is mainly about personal space. Personal space is known as one's own personal territory. According to the professor, personal space depends on two factors: intimacy and cultural standards. The professor first points out that intimacy is the closeness one person feels to another person. She gives an example of romantic relationships where people allow each other to enter their personal space. The second point she makes is about cultural standards. Cultural standards also influence how much personal space a person needs. As an example of cultural standards, she talks about population density. In low-density places like America, people usually keep a distance when walking with friends. In high-density places like Korea, girls often link arms with their friends.

 Test

B

Professor: As you all know, we use both nonverbal signals and verbal signals to communicate effectively. These also help us to deliver our messages clearly. Verbal signals are messages with words. Nonverbal signals are the facial expressions and the body language we use to support these verbal signals. These usually reveal how a person feels. In most cases, nonverbal signals work together with our verbal signals to show the meaning of our message to others. Like today, for example, while walking out of my house, I kissed my daughter on the cheek with a big smile and told her, "I love you." This sent a clear message to her because both my nonverbal and verbal signals demonstrated the same meaning. Sometimes, however, a nonverbal signal may not match up with the meaning of our verbal signals. Last week, for example, my son and I were building a tree house. He

accidentally hit my finger with the hammer, but in the moment of pain I didn't want to show my weakness. So, I told him, "I am fine." However, this was not true, as I was clearly in a lot of pain. My face was red and I was holding my finger in pain. This sent a conflicting message to my son and he didn't know what to do.

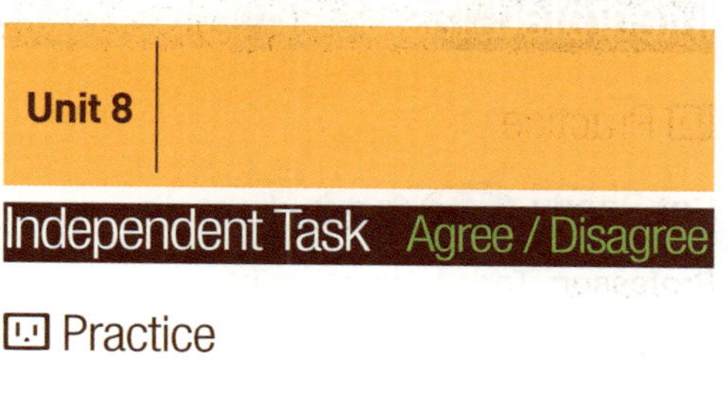

Practice

Check Your Response

☑ **Agree**   ☐ **Disagree**

I believe that people behave differently depending on what type of clothing they wear. There are two reasons why I believe this. One of the reasons is that looks have an effect on how people act. For example, when I wear baggy clothes, like hip-hop artists, I speak like rappers and walk differently. The other reason is that people tend to treat a person differently depending upon the type of clothing they wear. For instance, when I wear a nice suit, people seem to treat me with a lot of respect. In response, I also treat the other people politely. That's why I agree that people behave differently depending on what type of clothing they wear.

☐ **Agree**   ☑ **Disagree**

I believe that people do not behave differently depending on what type of clothing they wear. There are two reasons why I believe this. One of the reasons is that clothes themselves do not affect the way people act. People act differently because they feel different, not because of their clothes. The other reason is that most people do not care about what others think. For instance, I can walk right into a party wearing either a suit or sweat pants without a change in my behavior. My behavior does not change because of what I am wearing. That's why I disagree that people behave differently depending on what type of clothing they wear.

Integrated Task   General / Specific

Practice

Get Ready B-1 B-2

Professor: Today, we're going to talk about introverted and extroverted personality types and the different ways in which these types of people handle stress. How many of you would consider yourselves to be shy or outgoing? Do you know the difference? Well, introverts are people who like to spend time alone. When they get stressed out, they like to be alone and have space to think. An example of an introverted individual is my friend, Crystal. When Crystal is stressed out, she likes to stay home where she can read books, take baths, and have time to reflect on her own thoughts. She feels secure and relaxed when she has time to herself. If you can see a bit of yourself in Crystal, you may have an introverted personality type. On the other hand, extroverts are more sociable by nature and enjoy the company of others. When they get stressed out, they like to go out. My friend, Charles, is an example of an extroverted personality type. When Charles gets stressed out, he enjoys hanging out with his friends and being in large groups. After a long day at work, Charles enjoys playing basketball with his friends and going to parties. He finds it more comforting and enjoyable to be around others. If you are like Charles, then you would be considered an extrovert.

Check Your Response

The lecture is mainly about introverted and extroverted personality types, and the different ways that people who fit into these types handle stress. According to the professor, introverted people like to get rid of stress by spending time alone. He uses the example of his friend, Crystal, to talk about the introverted personality type. Crystal usually relieves stress by doing things alone such as reading books and meditating. He then talks about the way extroverted people like to relieve stress by going outside and hanging out with people. As an example of the extroverted personality type, he tells us about Charles. Charles relieves stress by playing basketball and hanging out with his friends at parties.

Test

B

Professor: Self-esteem is the evaluation of how we believe in or think of ourselves. What kind of self-esteem do you have? Would you consider yourself a confident person, or a very cautious person? Well, there are two types of self-esteem: high and low. Those with high self-esteem are confident in their own abilities. These traits are then played out in actions and behavior. Jack is an example of someone with high self-esteem. Last year, he didn't make his high school basketball team. Despite his failure, Jack was not discouraged and worked all summer to improve his skills and became team captain this year. He often told himself things like, "I'm sure I can do it" and "I'm so proud of myself." Jack did not let one failure affect his goals because he believed in himself. People with low self-esteem lack confidence and are likely to give up easily. They don't really like difficult challenges. Now, an example of someone with low self-esteem is Tyler. Tyler did not make the ice hockey team. He became so upset that he cried for more than two days. He told himself, "I am not good at it. I guess I'm not a talented hockey player." He did not even try to challenge himself. Two weeks later, Tyler sold his hockey uniform, and never returned to the ice rink.

Actual Test

Question 3 of 6

W: Finally! They're getting rid of all TVs in the common rooms. They were really disturbing and noisy.

M: Really? I liked having a TV in the common room. I relax by watching TV in the common room. If we don't have a TV in the common room, we will have to walk all the way to the main lounge. Besides, if we only have one TV, the whole dorm will have to share it, and I won't be able to watch what I want.

W: Don't you know that a common room is no place for a TV, It is meant to be a place to have quiet meetings and get work done.

M: Well... I don't think so. I always thought of it as a place to meet friends and watch TV shows together.

W: Hmm... When I had a team meeting with my friends the other night, I couldn't get any work done because of the noise from the TV.

M: That's true, but that's what we have the library for. The dorms should feel like home. The library is a much quieter and better place to study anyways.

W: I've never even seen people watching TV in the common room. It's just on all the time without anyone actually watching it.

Question 4 of 6

Professor: How many of you have siblings? Well, do you feel that people with younger siblings and people with older siblings have very different personalities? Let's look at the characteristics of the eldest. They often learn from their parents and try to behave in a similar fashion towards their younger siblings. As this happens, adults also expect the eldest to take care of the younger ones. This sometimes causes the eldest child to become a perfectionist. On the other hand, the last-born children have less pressure. As the youngest, last born children are loved by everyone. Therefore, they like to get attention from others. So, generally they become adventurous and outgoing individuals. Hmm... Let me talk about my two sons, Steve and Ted. Steve, the oldest son, always acts like a grown-up and has great responsibilities. Every day, he makes his bed perfectly, does chores around the house, and even washes the dishes for his mom. However, the youngest son, Ted, is so different from his brother. He thinks it's ok to leave without organizing the mess in his room. And he doesn't really feel bad about not helping his mom washing dishes. As the youngest in the family, he just likes to go out on adventures and to explore new places and meet new people.

Question 5 of 6

W: My roommate is so annoying!

M: Why? I thought you liked her.

W: I do, but it's final exam week and every time I try to study she starts singing!

M: Really? Does she just enjoy singing, or is there a reason she's singing so much?

W: Hmm... she's actually majoring in Music.

M: Well, if that's the case, you should try to talk to her directly. I'm sure she will understand.

W: Maybe, but I'm afraid things will get worse.

M: How so?

W: She's even loud on the weekends when she isn't practicing. She always brings over her friends to hang out. They are so loud. I haven't had a good sleep in weeks.

M: You should really talk to her.

W: I've tried, but she's so hard to talk to. She doesn't listen to me.

M: Try again, sometimes people don't listen the first time around.

W: Yeah, I might do that, but I wish I had more options.

M: Well, then you might try to ask a resident advisor for a room change.

W: Yeah, that might be a good idea too, but it is almost middle of the school year and I doubt they have any rooms available. It is also kind of annoying to, all of a sudden, pack and move all my things with mid-term exams coming up.

M: You should still try. It might be worth it in the end.

W: Yeah, I'll think about it.

Question 6 of 6

Professor: Okay class, who took the quiz this morning on short-term memory? Hmm...so you should know that short-term memory only lasts for a few minutes. However, long-term memory allows people to remember things for a long time. Do you also know that there are two types of long-term memory? They are declarative memory and procedural memory. Declarative memory allows people to remember what happened. Let's say Kevin is trying to memorize the order of the colors in a rainbow. He may use what we call a mnemonic device: "Roy G. Biv." Here, each letter is the first letter of a word. R for red, o for orange, y for yellow, etc. That way, he can remember the order of the rainbow's colors more easily and for a longer period of time. Studying for an exam using mnemonic devices can help one memorize and retain information longer. On the other hand, procedural memory allows people to remember things through a process, or how something happens. Learning how to ride a bicycle is a good example of the use of procedural memory. For example, Robert is trying to learn how to ride a bicycle. He keeps falling down and is having a difficult time picking up the skills. Like Robert, we also learn to ride a bicycle through practice and experience. Once you are able to ride a bicycle, you will always be able to in the future. This is because you do not only learn through what happens, but also through how it happens.

Winning TOEFL is a three-step series for beginning level students who are preparing for iBT TOEFL. Each step consists of four books: Listening, Reading, Speaking and Writing.

Winning TOEFL will help students be familiar with iBT TOEFL question types and provide opportunities to develop essential test skills through a step-by-step process.

Key Features of Winning TOEFL Speaking
- Focused practice for each task
- Step-by-step practice for the development of test skills
- Controlled and user-friendly guide to activities
- Transcripts for all listening exercises
- Full answer key including sample responses